THE MODERN
AMERICAN NOVELLA

THE MODERN
AMERICAN NOVELLA

edited by
A. Robert Lee

VISION PRESS · LONDON
ST. MARTIN'S PRESS · NEW YORK

Vision Press Ltd.
c/o Harper & Row Distributors Ltd.
Estover
Plymouth PL6 7PZ

and

St. Martin's Press, Inc.
175 Fifth Avenue
New York
N.Y. 10010

ISBN (UK) 0 85478 196 X
ISBN (US) 0 312 02424 X

Printed in Great Britain by
Billing & Sons Ltd, Worcester
Phototypeset by Galleon Photosetting,
Ipswich, Suffolk.
MCMLXXXIX

Contents

Introduction

by A. ROBERT LEE

Defining literary genres, notoriously, can be a road to perdition. Not only are hard and fast lines difficult to come by, but more even than usually the exception proves the rule or at the very least casts doubt upon any received consensus. To be reminded of the difficulties one has only to think of large categories like 'tragedy' or 'allegory' or 'epic', let alone smaller-scale forms like 'the short story' or 'the lyric' or even 'the essay'. Who, too, feels permanently or wholly persuaded by the great classic typologies, be they those set forth in Aristotle's *Poetics*, Sidney's *Apologie for Poetrie*, Coleridge's *Biographia Literaria*, Barthes's *Le degré zéro de l'écriture* or Northrop Frye's *Anatomy of Criticism*? Which is not for a moment to underplay the established force of these writings nor the utility in critical discussion of at least some ground rules and categorization. It is rather to fear the risk of foolishness in the manner of Polonius's listing of the varieties of drama for Hamlet.

Matters, too, take on added complication when the argument is put that genres are anything but innocent of history. They neither stand free of the times and values which shape them nor does one age's definition necessarily hold good for the next. Thus in historicizing genre we deny it status as a kind of meta-rhetoric, some fixed or transcendent mode of description. No doubt this is perfectly proper: Shakespeare's tragedies are not those prescribed by Aristotle, Coleridge's distinctions of 'imagination' and 'fancy' work best for his own age's poetry. But it makes life none too easy for the student of literary forms and kinds. Despite the come-back of an interest in 'typology' in the aftermath of structuralism, the old debate persists. Do we help or hinder in the understanding of a given text by assigning it to a generic category?

The novella has been especially implicated in these considerations. In the first place, it appears awkwardly betwixt and between—longer than the story and shorter than the novel, to put things at their most basic—an 'intermediate' narrative form often defined less by what it is than by what it is not. Its proponents are quick to point out the things it can do that its near-neighbours cannot. The novella can avail itself of a degree of detail which the short story must forego. At the same time it can offer a complication of setting or character or event without deploying the full sweep of time and place of the novel. But then on the other hand there are those who think the novella a chimera, simply a certain length of narrative in no way otherwise particularly distinct from the story or novel. Nor, too, to add a comparative note, can we always be sure that when the French speak of *la nouvelle* or the Italians of *la novella* or the Germans of *die Novelle* or Spanish-speakers of *la novela corta*, the reference is by any means a shared one. Be the association with, say, Flaubert or Boccaccio or Kleist or Cervantes, 'the novella' reads differently from within the values and assumptions of each different national literature.

Still another complication arises when we turn to the American novella. Few literatures have been quite so resistant to settled notions of form, and whether in prose or poetry. In the nineteenth-century this holds almost dramatically true. Does not, for instance, Hawthorne positively labour to convince us that he wrote romances rather than novels? What are we to make of Melville's talk of 'careful disorderliness' in his *Moby-Dick*? Are Emerson's 'essays' simply that, or sermons or forms of autobiography? What of Thoreau's *Walden*, self-narrative and no more? In Whitman's *Leaves of Grass* are we reading one poem or many, individual lyrics or a unified 'catalogue'? These, to be sure, are names from the American Renaissance, but the list extends—to Washington Irving's 'fake' histories, to Cooper's mythocentric Leatherstocking adventures, to Poe's first-person mysteries, and given their recovery, to Emily Dickinson's compact New England metaphysical poems. From beginnings like these, it hardly surprises that the novella, too, has taken on different hues and impulses.

And yet, perhaps oddly, it is with an American writer that the novella finds its best-known voice, namely Henry James.

His celebrated 'beautiful and blest *nouvelle*' seems, for a moment at least, to settle all debate about the form. Length, focus, scale, are to be released from the constraints of the regulation short story, yet without the need to go to the other extreme of full-fledged novel-writing. In some part, as has often and rightly been noted, James celebrated the novella because it suited his own publishing needs and personal compositional rhythms. He makes mention of virtually no other exponent of the form nor does he advance any specific theory as to its workings. But James's novellas we remember utterly, for him a genre heralded with enthusiasm and to be understood more in the doing than in the theory of what was being done.

Not that James was necessarily the first of American writers to make use of the form, but he presides as the titular presence. In him, a 'modern' par excellence, we see a necessary first begetter and ancestor. Hence the present collection is entitled *The Modern American Novella* and gives its opening focus to the author of the likes of *Daisy Miller*, *The Beast in the Jungle*, *The Turn of the Screw* and *In the Cage*. For this reason, too, Herman Melville is omitted, both his *Israel Potter: or, Fifty Years of Exile* (1855) and his *Billy Budd, Sailor* (1888-91). Neither of these narratives yields anything but major imaginative fare, though the story of 'welkin-eyed' Billy caught in a fatal triangulation with Claggart and Vere has prevailed far more so than that of the exiled mariner who returns to his decline and death in post-Revolutionary America. Both amount to texts indispensable in a total consideration of the American novella, but both might genuinely be best regarded as belonging to a pre-modern era.

Henry James, then, offers a first point of departure, a classic adept in the novella from whom to take bearings. In his opening essay Michael Irwin pays James this clear due, an acknowledgement of the sheer virtuosity of 'the master'. But he also suggests grounds for a certain unease. Could not that very same virtuosity—the novella as at every turn too conscious of itself as a narrative art-form—be disenabling? James, time and again, shows himself interested in the 'idea' of a given situation to the point where he seems less concerned to allow it resolution in 'life' as it were. Just as many of the protagonists in his novellas, notably Winterbourne, or the governess in *The Turn of the Screw*, or John Marcher, or the heroine of *In the Cage*, embody (if that

9

is a right word for it) abnegation, so his story-telling can arguably engage in a reflexivity at its own expense. It may well be that James saw in his own most 'blest' of forms simply too good a thing, an occasion to muse and embroider upon the art of the novella rather than to make final the story any given novella is telling. Yet only so consummate a fiction-writer would pose that kind of worry.

No such considerations arise in the case of Stephen Crane's *The Red Badge of Courage*, at least not so if the arguments I make for its workings are at all apt. Crane's key phrase 'inside a moving box', his metaphor for the Union regiment in which Henry Fleming serves as an enlistee during the American Civil War, I suggest also holds as a way of understanding the novella itself. Crane, to be sure, wrote one of the unmistakable landmarks of war-fiction, arms and the man rarely better made over into narrative—for all the irony that Crane himself never took part in combat. But *The Red Badge* also becomes the very thing it seeks to narrate, a 'box' which draws in and compels the reader to move with Henry Fleming from calm to panic, innocence to experience. Its main operative metaphors and energies have an almost geometric force, enclosing us as they enclose 'the youth' who achieves an ironic manhood by becoming a veteran soldier.

A different kind of enclosure marks the life and fate of Edna Pontellier in Kate Chopin's *The Awakening*. That, at any rate, gives Dorothy Goldman her focus in her strongly feminist reading of the book. She sees it as a novella of discovery and a drift towards death in the face of Edna's inability to make good in life on the import of her discoveries. One way through might have been through the life-affirmation to be gained from art. So, in fact, runs the argument in Sharon Shaloo's consideration of the four *Old New York* novellas of Edith Wharton. As Wharton uses her novellas to portray creative fulfilment, so, too, they portray the matching route for their protagonists into sexual and emotional fulfilment.

On Harold Beaver's interpretation, the novellas of Nathanael West—*The Dream Life of Balso Snell, Miss Lonelyhearts, A Cool Million* and *The Day of the Locust*—make a distinct virtue of their brevity, a kind of strip cartoon story-telling marked out by one-liners, jumps and dissolves. To enter a West novella is to respond to American baroque, a dark, filmic chamber of horrors in which distortion becomes the very name of the game. Hemingway's *The Old Man and the Sea* and Faulkner's 'The Bear', two novella-length pieces by two of America's prime fiction-writers, give David Timms his bases for a comparison which presses outwards to a consideration of the generic implications of the form. The first he designates 'a model novella', while the second he ponders as a narrative which raises the issue of what happens when 'complications' of time and space enter the story-telling.

Faulkner's 'The Bear' points southwards into the 'mythical kingdom' of Yoknapatawpha. And it is that region, indeed the Old South at large, that Peter Messent shows to have given a whole line of major American novellas. In linking work by Andrew Lytle, Robert Penn Warren, William Styron, Truman Capote, Barry Hannah, Eudora Welty, Katherine Anne Porter and Carson McCullers, he analyses both the Faulknerian legacy of 'history' and the extraordinary propensity of the region to express itself fictionally in the novella form.

Which brings the collection to two crucial early contemporaries, J. D. Salinger and Saul Bellow. For David Seed, Salinger's *The Catcher in the Rye* and the surrounding Glass family novellas (most notably *Franny and Zooey*) could not more border on the self-reflexive, parables of a creative-artistic dynasty told in forms which not unproblematically acknowledge their own begetting. He suggests how we might best take the measure of 'this narrative posture'. Michael Glenday, on the other hand, looks at the novellas of a writer who has made it his business to explore 'American reality' with no holds barred. Not for Bellow the ways of the self-reflexive or self-referential. Whether an early novella like *Seize the Day* or one of later vintage like *What Kind of Day Did You Have?* Bellow also matches his aesthetic with his thematic interests, that of a resolute if infinitely various and adroitly conjured realism.

The present collection offers no definitive answers as to the novella-form itself nor the especial 'Americanness' of the American novella. But it does touch on both, sometimes explicitly and at others tacitly. What I hope equally shows through at all times is how important and how enduring the novella has been in American literature, a small-scale form from a culture

11

whose imaginative offerings have usually thought to be given to largeness. From James onwards the novella has taken its place in American literary history, but rarely with the acknowledgement that it yields a tradition in its own terms. *The Modern American Novella* seeks to put that to rights.

1

Henry James and the Vague *Nouvelle*

by MICHAEL IRWIN

1

The aspiring writer, or student of literary forms, interested in the potentialities of the novella,[1] would turn naturally to Henry James. Who better to give guidance as to its nature and scope than the author who praised so enthusiastically 'the beautiful and blest *nouvelle*'?[2] Such theoretical comment as James offers, however, proves teasingly unspecific. In defining the genre he places great emphasis on its lower limit; he is less concerned with distinguishing the novella from the novel than with celebrating the freedom it affords, in 'length and breadth', as contrasted to the constraints of the short story, with its 'hard-and-fast' 6,000 to 8,000 words. The larger form can allow for 'the idea happily *developed*', for organic shape.

There is a countervailing stress on economy, 'a strong brevity and lucidity'. Though James does not pursue the point at the theoretical level, analysis of his work in the genre will show the considerations likely to be involved. Typically a James novella will be monocentric, the elaboration of a single issue. The cast-list is likely to be small. Most of the component scenes will feature two characters only. The action may be confined, or largely confined, to a single arena—perhaps an arena implied in the very title of the story, as in *The Pension Beaurepas*, *The Birthplace* or *In the Cage*.

All this sounds orthodox enough. In practice, however, one of the characteristics glanced at above becomes so curiously predominant as to give James's novellas an idiosyncratic cast. ·The root of the oddity is the word 'idea', several times reiterated in relevant Prefaces. In casual discussion one speaks of 'an idea for a short story', when what is at issue is the plot or situation that has provided the author's starting-point. The term could be used in relation to an action-packed yarn. But for James the 'idea' is likely to be an abstract idea—a concept. The story that dramatizes it will take place largely inside the head of the principal character. He or she will be striving to solve a puzzle, or to reach a correct understanding; it is this attempt that constitutes the 'action'. Does the governess in *The Turn of the Screw* see ghosts, or are the apparitions projected from her sub-consciousness? Are Daisy Miller and Pandora what they appear to the young men who uneasily observe them? Is Captain Everard the romantic figure he seems to be when seen through the bars of the Cage? Like the literary critics in *The Figure in the Carpet* the characters concerned are 'engaged in a test'. And as in that case, to borrow James's own words, 'The reader is, on the evidence, left to conclude.'

But this exercise is a complex one. James uses the extra 'breadth' of the novella not for physical description or circumstantial thickening but for more detailed analysis of the internal drama. He 'develops' it with an intensity, a scrupulosity, that seems to demand a correspondingly rigorous response on the reader's side. Yet various of the author's habits of thought or technique go far towards frustrating such a response. The result is a mode of fiction often intriguing, but curiously elusive and indistinct. The reader cannot 'on the evidence . . . conclude', because the evidence is inadequate or questionable. Some of the best-known novellas are elliptical exercises in ambiguity, tantalizing as a Mobius strip.[3]

2

The stories that take an American visitor to Europe, or a European to America, run the risk inherent in any comedy (or tragi-comedy) of manners; as manners alter with the passage of time, so meaning will be blurred or lost. The deportment of James's new arrivals is to be judged, or misjudged, in terms of conformity to 'the done thing'. But sight-lines have shifted so far that it can be difficult to discern what 'the done thing' was—still more to decide whether it was what it should have been. In a comparable literary predicament Jane Austen, for one, contrived to create a sense of social context seemingly sufficient to enable us to judge what might constitute (say) 'vulgarity' or 'impropriety'. Arguably James provides a comparable insight into relevant standards and conventions in his full-length novels. In the novellas, however, the length is insufficient to provide for many such promptings, while breadth is rarely sacrificed to them. The well-disposed reader can only accept the social assumptions that seem to prevail within the milieu described. As a corollary, of course, various responses natural to our own period must be suppressed as anachronistic.

Accommodations of this sort are not difficult; the serious reader expects to pay some such admission-fee to a work of literature from the past. What can seem disconcerting in the case of some of James's society novellas is their tendency to work their way—as towards a surprise ending—to the very view that the reader has loyally suppressed. What judgement are we to pass on Daisy Miller? How indiscreet, or dubious, is her conduct? Our present-day vantage-point permits no sensible conclusion; the situation, in all its aspects, is too remote. We are obliged to make what we can of the information provided in the story itself if we are to decide what would have been reasonable at that time and in that place.

The obvious source of authority would seem to be Winterbourne. It is not merely that his judgements are more generous than those of the society within which he moves; they are the only liberal judgements to which the reader is given access. In any case he gets certain things manifestly right. His concern that Daisy's midnight trip to the Colosseum will give her Roman fever looks fussily valetudinarian to the modern eye. But Daisy promptly justifies his forebodings by catching the illness and dying of it. Earlier in the story he points out to her that Giovanelli 'would never have proposed to a young lady of this country to walk about the streets of Rome with him'. We have to assume that the claim is correct—and it seems a relevant one. Since Winterbourne is 'right' on such practical issues, and seems to be our only available guide through the intricacies of a remote and enclosed society, we tend to accept his interpretations concerning issues less categorical. He does not dissent from his aunt's implied claim that it is possible to recognize 'regular Roman fortune-hunters of the inferior sort'. It would seem that Giovanelli has some of the distinguishing marks of this species: an 'obsequious' manner, flowers in the button-hole, a 'coxcombical' regard for personal appearance. 'Do you mean to speak to that thing?' is Winterbourne's question to Daisy when he first sets eyes on her Italian friend. Some conversation with him mitigates the initial revulsion, but the American still finds it 'deeply disgusting' that Daisy has not 'instinctively discriminated against such a type'. An occasional phrase— 'Winterbourne flattered himself he had taken his measure'; 'a presumably low-lived foreigner'—hints that these verdicts are premature, but what does not seem to be in doubt is the existence of a 'type' that can be identified by these criteria or something very like them. When Winterbourne later tries to take a more generous view of Giovanelli, the best he can manage is 'shiny—but to do him justice, not greasy'. Since Daisy, whose judgement is precisely what is in question, is the only person to have a more generous opinion of Giovanelli, we are pretty well obliged to assent to Winterbourne's estimate; there is no basis for an alternative assessment. We discount our reservations as twentieth-century irrelevancies. Yet in the upshot Giovanelli comes to display better manners and truer feeling than his rival. It is he who behaves magnanimously at Daisy's funeral. Winterbourne can only respond 'with a grace inferior to his friend's'.

With respect to Giovanelli, then, the reader is brought to a position originally ruled out by the pressures of the story itself. It is not our prejudices that have been overcome but those of Winterbourne—and possibly of James himself. For though the letter of the text rebukes Winterbourne's dismissal of Giovanelli, the spirit of it does not. The Italian is a subordinate element in the novella—part of the machinery. His feelings are represented only to the extent that they induce him to reveal more about his relationship with Daisy. Winterbourne offers neither explanations nor apologies in return for these confidences, but there is no authorial comment, even of an indirect kind, on the omission. In effect the story seems to endorse, after all, Winterbourne's assumption that Giovanelli isn't 'interesting' enough to deserve them; he is one of life's minor characters.

The point is far from being merely a formal one. The novella invites us to reach towards some delicate moral conclusions concerning Daisy's conduct and the various reactions to it. We are enabled to see that Winterbourne's assessment is faulty, but are given access to no reference outside it. The central 'idea' can be tricked out so tantalizingly because it is defined only within a circular system of relative judgements.

There are comparable problems in other 'international' stories. Repeatedly James asks us to interest ourselves in the aspects of his characters that many of us nowadays would find least appealing. Money and status loom large, work and ability do not. Again, the modern reader can accept this system of values in effect as a convention—only to find, in many cases, that the point of the narrative is to undermine that very convention. For example, Jackson Lemon is drawn to Lady Barbarina because he likes 'her type':

> she seemed to him to have a part of the history of England in her blood; she was a *résumé* of generations of privileged people, and of centuries of rich country-life.

He woos her not as an individual he knows and loves, but as a representative of tradition and 'race'. Transplanted to New York his bride proves shallow-brained and surly. Lemon is surprised and disappointed, but the modern reader can hardly share these feelings. Only as a concession to the apparent requirements of the story have we subdued the assumption that this is a courtship ill-founded and foolishly conducted.

Moreover, in this novella James comes confusingly close to endorsing the values his narrative seems designed to reprobate. Like Winterbourne, Lemon goes wrong through thinking too crudely in categories—in this case categories of tradition and race. But the story itself involves judgements of just this kind. It attempts to convey general truths about the differences between London and New York 'society' and the pitfalls of Anglo-American marriages. In short, it is a contradiction—a generic work about the dangers of thinking generically. To confuse matters further, Lemon's damaging readiness to give primacy to social status seems to be a weakness that his creator shares.

But for his inheritance Lemon would, it seems, be an outstanding doctor; blessed with money he turns his interest to research. But this aspect of his life is given scant attention in the narrative. The best James can manage is: 'Jackson Lemon was making some researches, just now, which took up a great deal of his time . . .'. The author's interest in Lemon is like Lemon's interest in Lady Barbarina: overwhelmingly social. It is as if James misses the point of his own story.

In *Pandora* there is yet another implicit rebuke for generic thinking. When Vogelstein asks Mrs. Dangerfield about Pandora's social position, he is teased: 'Oh, social position . . . What big expressions you use!' A couple of years of American experience later he asks his friend Mrs. Bonnycastle about the social position of Mrs. Steuben, only to be greeted with 'mocking laughter'. He must learn his lesson: '. . . how little one could tell, after all, in America, who people were!' The story would seem at this stage to be an argument for the greater variety and individuality of American life as against the arid stereotyping of the European tradition. But this impression proves misleading. Pandora is to be found interesting not as an individual, but as 'the new type', 'the self-made girl'. A couple of pages are devoted to a detailed, if approximate, definition of this 'type'. After all, America *has* a class system: Vogelstein's only mistake has been to expect it to conform to the European pattern.

This seeming contradiction in the story cuts awkwardly deep at its close. Attracted to Pandora despite himself Count Otto begins to wonder whether she might not, despite everything, make a good wife for a diplomat—even a diplomat such as himself. But he is not allowed to drift far in the direction of temptation. It transpires that Pandora has been engaged since the age of 16 to a Mr. Bellamy from Utica. Thanks to her direct appeal to the President this gentleman is appointed Minister to Holland. Pandora promptly marries the diplomat she herself has been instrumental in promoting.

An initial reaction is likely to be that the laugh is on Vogelstein. How little this arch-conservative understands the freedom of the United States, where 'the silver spoon of social opportunity' can be grasped 'by honest exertion'. But further reflection undermines the easy irony. Should so considerable a post be dependent upon the skill with which a pretty girl can chat up the President at a party? Does this activity qualify as 'honest exertion'? This glimpse of the workings of the American system scarcely provides a secure base from which to mock the German one. In theory, of course, the satirical implications could be two-edged: James could be making the point that the slap-happy American approach is after all no less rational or meritocratic than its European counterpart. But the tenor of the narrative surely suggests that we should view these procedures as equally reasonable, not as equally senseless or corrupt. In any case, the point scarcely signifies. Whether James has failed to see how dubious Pandora's achievement appears, or whether (improbably) he is poking fun at the very notion of diplomatic and social status, the framework within which the ironic quizzicalities work has begun to collapse. A comedy centrally concerned with someone learning the ropes cannot satisfactorily conclude that ropes are not worth learning, or that one rope is indistinguishable from another.

3

In isolation the argument of the preceding section is of limited interest. It is not uncommon for a novelist to lapse into implied contradiction. Which of us can confidently lay claim to total consistency? The intriguing thing in James's case is that paradoxes of this kind are symptomatic of a more general tendency. He does not drift into radical ambiguities; it is his habit to engender them.

The tendency is amply discernible at the level of technique— in his dialogue, for example. Often the 'development of the idea' in a given novella entails extended passages of elucidatory discussion. The characters press towards understanding or definition. This seems, at any rate, to be the process the author is dramatizing. But the numerous (and notorious) oddities of Jamesian dialogue make for a very different effect. These idio-syncrasies include unfinished sentences, a copious use of abstract nouns, and a strangely uneasy handling of the vernacu-lar. Commonplace phrases are put between inverted commas, as though to suggest either that the meaning conveyed can be only approximate, or that the speaker is resorting to a form of speech with which he is not comfortable. Looseness of metaphor contributes to the precariousness of the attempts at communication:

> 'They came down.'
> His friends were all interest. 'Ah! They came down?'
> 'Heavy. They brought *me* down. That's *why*—'
> 'Why you are down?' Mrs. Hayes sweetly demanded.
> 'Ah, but my dear man', her husband interposed, 'you're not down; you're *up*! You're only up a different tree, but you're up at the tip-top.'
> 'You mean I take it too high?'
> 'That's exactly the question,' the young man answered; 'and the possibility, as matching your first danger, is just what we felt we couldn't, if you didn't mind, miss the measure of.'
>
> (*The Birthplace*)[4]

The reader who suffers some twinges of uncertainty on tackling such a passage as this can take consolation from the fact that James's characters often puzzle one another. Requests for clarification are commonplace. Sometimes a remark may need an explanatory gloss:

> 'But we have a sort of place we go to—an hour from Euston. That's one of the reasons.'
> 'One of the reasons?'   •
> 'Why my books are so bad.' (*The Lesson of the Master*)

More frequently a floating pronoun can be misconstrued:

> 'And now you quite like it?' I risked.
> 'My work?'
> 'Your secret. It's the same thing.' (*The Figure in the Carpet*)[5]

In quite a number of cases one or more of the characters concerned will be deliberately dealing in evasion or insinuation. It's easy to sympathize with Bessie Alden's complaint: ' "I have never heard in the course of five minutes," she said, "so many hints and innuendoes. I wish you would tell me in plain English what you mean" ' (*An International Episode*).

These idiosyncrasies of dialogue are, of course, a notable characteristic of the full-length novels. But in that larger context (to generalize) they blur only slightly the outlines of a situation that gradually defines itself through the course of the extended narrative. In the novellas, where economy demands that the dialogue does much of the expository work, the case is rather different. The equivocations and obfuscations may not seem to derive from the complexity of the situation that is being dramatized. They may rather be felt to generate the very mystery or uncertainty that in theory is generating them.

In certain instances this is manifestly the author's technique. When the governess in *The Turn of the Screw* exclaims 'I don't know what I *don't* see—what I *don't* fear!' the purposefulness of the double negation would be plain even without James's prefatory explanations. In a tale of the supernatural, specificity is limiting: the reader is left to imagine his or her personal worst. If this is one kind of special case, perhaps *The Figure in the Carpet* is another. Early in the tale James seems deliberately to mock one of his own brands of imprecision. The narrator, who is to review a novel by Hugh Vereker, is urged by George Corvick, an admirer of Vereker, not to be 'silly':

> 'Silly—about Vereker! Why what do I ever find him but awfully clever?'
> 'Well, what's that but silly? What on earth does "awfully clever" mean? For God's sake try to get *at* him.'

Attempting to press the case Corvick can only manage:

> '. . . he gives me a pleasure so rare; the sense of'—he mused a little—'something or other.'
> I wondered again. 'The sense, pray, of what?'
> 'My dear man, that's just what I want *you* to say!'

Like the governess at Bly, the main characters in this novella are to become obsessed with the pursuit of something that may not exist and that cannot be adequately defined. What they try to discern in Vereker's work is variously described as 'my little point', 'my great affair', 'my idea', 'this little trick of mine', 'an idea in my work', 'the finest fullest intention of the lot', 'the organ of life', 'the very string . . . that my pearls are strung on', and 'something like a complex figure in a Persian carpet'. In his Preface James alludes to it as Vereker's 'undiscovered, not to say undiscoverable, secret'. It affords reasonable sport within the story, but surely has the potentiality also of beguiling the reader into joining the game—as in *The Turn of the Screw*. To reflect on this polymorphous nebulosity in respect of an imaginary author is an activity very much akin to inventing your own ghost. It has more of the practical in it only to the extent that the investigation might be applied to the work of James himself.

These two novellas can usefully be considered alongside a puzzle-piece of a rather different kind—*The Beast in the Jungle*. Here, too, the central figure is possessed by an 'idea'—in this case the notion of being reserved for some rare, terrible, 'possibly annihilating' fate. The difference is that this idea goes beyond verbal ambiguity or morbid imaginings; it translates into a tragic actuality. The reader, it would seem, is in a position to measure John Marcher's obsession against the climactic realization it prefigures. Once more, however, though for complex reasons, the relationship between inner and outer worlds proves problematic.

Though an ingenious early flashback modifies the problem by ten years, this novella has to span an entire career—in effect a lifetime—passed in the shadow of this mortal dread. Yet ninety-nine per cent of all Marcher's doings are disposed of in a single parenthesis about

> the forms he went through—those of his little office under Government, those of caring for his patrimony, for his library, for his garden in the country, for the people in London whose invitations he accepted and repaid—.

This brisk clearing of the ground could be reasonable enough: the 'economy' of the Jamesian novella frequently involves disproportioning of this kind, if not of this degree—a bleaching out of the extraneous in the interests of concentration upon a particular subject. As a matter of narrative convention, then, we can accept that Marcher's life consists almost solely of anxious reflection about his 'inevitable topic' and anxious conversation with May Bartram upon the same theme. But this maniacal self-absorption is acceptable *only* in terms of convention. If a real-life acquaintance carried on like Marcher we would regard him as a tiresome bore, perhaps as a sick man. *The Beast in the Jungle* can be taken seriously only to the extent that the protagonist and his plight have dignity. Hence we do not take Marcher's solipsism literally. The assumption is that the dread constantly in his mind and conversation is a metaphor— a means of dramatizing some fear more substantial but too deep-rooted and disguised to be accessible to direct narrative demonstration. In the event, however, what seemed mere convention is translated into substance—into the very solution of the mystery that has darkened Marcher's life. His tragedy is that he has failed to live or love, precisely because of his egotistical preoccupation with a fear of tragedy. It would appear, with hindsight, that the story has been realistic rather than stylized. Marcher has presumably behaved literally as James represents him behaving—thinking and talking (at a serious level) of nothing but his dread of impending catastrophe. In a spiritual sense he has died of hypochondria. On the assumption that something more sophisticated than this was at issue, many a reader will have suppressed the thought that May Bartram should simply tell Marcher to snap out of it. In retrospect this looks, after all, like good advice.

While in tone and import, then, this novella seems a good deal more serious than *The Turn of the Screw* or *The Figure in the Carpet*, the mystery at its heart, as in those cases, dissolves into artifice.[6] The 'solution' is disappointing because the story promises much more. There is power in the narrative of a parabolic kind. By inversion Marcher might stand for the Artist who leaves his life unlived as he waits for some crisis of creativity (as opposed to the destruction that is dreaded here). Alternatively he could be the repressed homosexual, so much in dread of his deeper impulses that he is reduced to eking out a pallid imitation of a heterosexual relationship to enable him 'to pass for a man iike another'. In order for the potentiality of the novella to be fulfilled, the ending would have to be sufficiently open to accommodate and develop interpretative possibilities of some such colour. Instead it presents an explanation that seems to derive not from the essential 'idea', but from the narrative artifice employed to dramatize that idea. A novella that offered an intriguingly distorted reflection of a problem from the real world proves neatly, but disappointingly, reflexive.

4

In the Cage is a novella more substantial, more dense in texture, than most of James's work in the genre. Unusually it features a sub-plot; and by a skilful narrative sleight the resolution of this story, concerning Mrs. Jordan, contributes to the resolution of the heroine's. It does so, moreover, by providing an unexpected opportunity for the protagonist to check her carefully nurtured fantasy against external information. In other ways, too, the outside world is kept in view. There is economic detail: the heroine borrows novels from the library at a ha'penny a day; a move from Mayfair to Chalk Farm would save her nearly three shillings in rent. Again, part of the 'breadth' of the novella is used to convey a sense of physical context. The shop which holds the 'cage' is 'pervaded . . . by the presence of hams, cheese, dried fish, soap, varnish, paraffin . . .'. The heroine must work 'where Mr. Buckton's elbow could freely enter her right side and the counter-clerk's breathing—he had something the matter with his nose—pervade her left ear'. Mrs. Jordan is afflicted with 'extraordinarily protrusive teeth'. Her 'little parlour' seems to contain no more than 'teacups and a pewter pot, and a very black little fire, and a paraffin lamp without a shade'.

Such detail is important in the story as exemplifying the dinginess in the heroine's life that makes her retreat into a world of unreality. The conception is a powerful one. Here is a girl with a strong romantic imagination, who shrinks from the occupation forced upon her by economic necessity. Yet that very occupation throws her into daily contact with the wealthy, with elegant men and women whose mysterious telegrams apparently promote subtle transactions and sinful pleasures. Her imagination is stimulated to excess in this 'world of whiffs and glimpses'. Skilled at recognizing 'types' and interpreting the coded language of telegraphy, she reads meanings everywhere. In particular she fabricates a complex relationship between herself and Captain Everard, a regular customer, from the merest conversational fragments—a word of greeting, a remark about the weather:

> . . . it fed her fancy that no form of intercourse so transcendent and distilled had ever been established on earth. Everything, so far as they chose to consider it so, might mean almost anything.

Altogether James has posed himself a difficult challenge. The more strongly imaged outer world provides a criterion against which to test the heroine's 'idea'. At the same time the elusiveness, the precariousness, of that inner life, where 'everything might mean almost anything', becomes central, becomes thematic. The author sympathizes with his heroine, paying tribute to 'our young friend's native distinction, her refinement of personal grain, of heredity, of pride'; but in displaying her modes of perception and response, in writing through them, he is plainly concerned to show how her imaginative vision distorts the reality it transcends.

Three aspects of the story bring the girl into direct engagement with other people: her relationships with Mrs. Jordan and with Mr. Mudge, and her one conversation with Captain Everard outside the 'cage'. Any of the encounters concerned might produce jagged realities that would puncture the heroine's imaginings. The conversations with Mrs. Jordan, however, save for the climactic one, are safely negotiated because this lady, too, lives out certain fantasies. Like 'our young friend', and for very similar reasons, she will deal in hints and equivocations, romanticizing her daily doings and exaggerating her prospects. The two women can gingerly collaborate in an exchange of home-made society gossip.

The meeting with Captain Everard poses problems of quite a different order. His telegrams suggest to the reader a somewhat shady, if not seedy, character. What the heroine sees as his 'exquisite' good humour does not stop him from 'smoking in her face'. It would not be easy, in any case, to guess how such a person would respond to the girl outside her cage; what makes it actually impossible is our lack of knowledge concerning the girl herself. Her anonymity extends to her appearance. We have been told that she 'usually struck' Mrs. Jordan as 'pretty', but this is not self-evidently a striking compliment. To place the scene in the park we need a clearer sense of how she would appear to Captain Everard's eyes. The only safe conclusion, 'not too bad', leaves a wide margin of ambiguity round the situation. We know too little about either of the characters to be able to guess the likely outcome.

In what is *said*, however—and this is an impressive aspect of the novella—James does not simply take refuge in ambiguities. He goes at any rate halfway towards meeting the challenge he has set himself. The girl from the post-office, desperately anxious that there should be no hint of misconstruction or 'vulgarity', declares her position as directly as she can. Conscious of the risk she runs in doing so, she finds that very risk exhilarating. When she has described her sense that there is something between them, and exclaimed 'I'd do anything for you', she is exalted:

> Never in her life had she known anything so high and fine as this, just letting him have it and bravely and magnificently leaving it. Didn't the place, the associations and circumstances, perfectly make it sound what it was not? and wasn't that exactly the beauty?

Her fantasy, then, is placed squarely at the mercy of the realities of Captain Everard. But James, as though unwilling, after all, to face the harshness of the resolution that is threatened, keeps the Captain's responses, whether of words or gesture, at a level that leaves them assimilable to the girl's own version of the relationship. He does not snub her, he does not try to seduce her, he does not expostulate or make hurried excuses and leave. In fact it is she who breaks off the encounter with the touchingly futile reassurance 'I won't abandon you!' The reader, like the girl herself, has learned little more about the plausibility of her imaginings. Most of Everard's comments are vapid or fragmentary. He does agree that her knowledge of his situation has been the thing between them, but this vague phrase is all that sustains her interpretation of their relationship. On the other hand he says nothing that would seriously impair her illusions. James shirks his self-imposed challenge to the extent that he makes the conversation with Captain Everard pose her no serious problem. It is not that the man's reactions are implausible; we lack the knowledge that would enable us to pass such a judgement. We have seen him very largely through the heroine's imaginings. But when the interview leaves those imaginings essentially intact, the major question the text has invited us to try to answer takes on a different status. The ambiguity attaching to the heroine's subjective view of the Captain now becomes an ambiguity in the story proper. James has under-written it—insulated the girl from reality. Even when she is outside the cage he allows her (and the reader) no more than 'whiffs and glimpses'.

Her relationship with Mr. Mudge poses problems that the

author cannot evade so easily. She is, after all, engaged to the man, and hence compelled to consider, at the level of practical reality, how far she can accommodate his personality and tastes. James struggles here. Unless Mudge has some positive qualities the girl's attachment will seem merely materialistic. But if he is too impressive a figure her devotion to the Captain will smack of infidelity. James tries to be fair to him. He is allowed certain unexpected reserves of character, as well as the courage and decisiveness that enable him to deal with the drunken soldier. But neither the heroine nor the author seems able to go beyond a grudging respect for him. Their distaste is repeatedly hinted: Mudge is 'oleaginous' and takes notes in a 'greasy' pocket-book. His fiancée tells him that he is 'awfully inferior' to Captain Everard, and certainly considers him inferior to herself: 'There were times when she wondered how in the world she could bear him, how she could bear any man so smugly unconscious of the immensity of her difference.'

Presumably to mitigate the element of betrayal in the girl's conduct James has her tell Mudge about her relationship with Captain Everard, and even win his tacit assent to it. But the conversation that produces the required understanding is a strained affair. James has failed to find a consistent speech-style for Mudge, and the dialogue in question is made possible only by that very failure. Mudge, and the heroine's relationship with him, are at best no more than hazily imaginable.

The girl's attitude to her husband-to-be typifies her passionate snobbery. In her final conversation with Mrs. Drake she cannot resist a gibe at the friend who has been reduced to marrying Lady Bardeen's butler. Her own future husband, she explains, is only a grocer 'so that I'm afraid that, with the set you've got into, you won't see your way to keep up our friendship.' Mrs. Jordan sees through this malicious euphemism at once, and begins to cry, accusing the girl of 'cooling off'. Reconciliatory gestures are made, but we learn that 'our young lady' 'by no means saw herself sitting down, as she might say, to the same table with Mr. Drake.' She can have this reaction at the very moment of reflecting, with less exclusivity: 'Reality, for the poor things they both were, could only be ugliness and obscurity, could never be the escape, the rise.'

The snobbery cannot be passed over, since it relates directly

to the central concerns of the story. We are invited to take an
interest in the heroine's rich imaginative doings, which contrast
so sharply with her diurnal drudgeries. She sees the affair
between Lady Bradeen and Captain Everard as 'their high
encounter with life, their large and complicated game'. Yet at
the close of the story this relationship is shown—through
further 'whiffs and glimpses'—to have been a pretty dubious
piece of adventurism. Is not the corollary that the heroine, for
all her 'refinement of personal grain', has an imagination rather
crudely conditioned by social snobbery? Is it not tainted, even,
by 'vulgarity'? She herself does not seem to take this point.
What is more disturbing is that James does not seem to take it
either. His conclusion seems too small in scale for the story he
has told. He may think, with his heroine, that her world (which
is virtually the whole world of H. G. Wells) 'could only be
ugliness and obscurity', but should not the shoddiness of her
dream life be more emphatically acknowledged?

5

An obvious answer to the misgivings outlined above would be
along these lines: 'James's interest is in the imaginative life *per
se*, in the "idea", rather than in the external world to which the
idea relates.' In the novels, however, the idea, or ideal, is
characteristically thrust into painful comparison with reality;
this seems to be the very business James is about. It is the more
disconcerting, therefore, to find that in the novellas the
characters are so often impotent, shirking the encounter with
reality and allowing experience to dissolve into theory. In a
curious way their preference for sucking an idea rather than
biting on it reflects James's procedure as narrator. He will not
allow them to reach a conclusion.[7] He preserves the inviolability
of the 'idea' by refusal to think it through, by various minor
habits of obfuscation, but above all by a technique of reflexivity.
The idea cannot be considered independently of the story that
dramatizes it, because it is actually derived from the narrative
artifices involved in the telling of that story. The reaction to this
mode of composition will no doubt differ sharply from reader to
reader according to temperament. For some the circularity of
this type of novella will seem peculiarly rewarding as offering

for contemplation and re-contemplation an 'idea' endlessly ambiguous. For others there may be rather the sense that a problem thus produced and sustained is really a pseudo-problem. Beyond a certain point they may even be irritated by its ambiguities, as by the instability of a wobbling table.

NOTES

1. Despite James's reference to the 'nouvelle' the least problematic of the available terms would seem to be 'novella'. See Gerald Gillespie's 'Novelle, Nouvelle, Novella, Short Novel?—A Review of Terms', *Neophilologus*, 50–1 (1967), and J. H. E. Paine, *Theory and Criticism of the Novella* (Bonn: Bouvier 1979), p. 64.

2. The theoretical comments here are quoted from James's Preface to Volume XV of Scribner's New York Edition of his collected works.

3. Compare Judith Leibowitz, *Narrative Purpose in the Novella* (The Hague: Mouton, 1974), who suggests (p. 16) that the novella characteristically involves 'outward expansion from a limited focus. . .'. My argument is that in most of his novellas James provides only an illusion of such 'outward expansion', since their suggestiveness is reflexive.

4. The examples that follow are drawn from a range of James's novellas, without regard to date of composition. I agree with Ralf Norrman that 'most, if not all, of the idiosyncrasies of the late style exist in embryonic form in the early style.' See *The Insecure World of Henry James's Fiction* (London: Macmillan, 1982), p. 3.

5. Norrman (see above) devotes a whole chapter to 'Referential Ambiguity in Pronouns' in *The Golden Bowl* alone.

6. In her *Forms of the Modern Novella* (Chicago: University of Chicago Press, 1975) Mary Doyle Springer claims (p. 127) that 'we are bound to be with . . . Marcher as he flings himself, "face down, on the tomb" '. Against this Paine argues (op. cit., p. 87) 'that by that point many readers are so disgusted with him that they revel in his demise'. I would suggest that neither kind of emotion is appropriate, since the ending has reduced Marcher from human being to device.

7. Norrman would attribute this inconclusiveness to James's thoroughgoing chiasticism—the tendency 'to *complement* any given statement with its own inversion. . .' (op. cit., p. 187). I am sorry that I did not come across this interesting study until after the completion of my own essay. The emphasis in Norrman's 'Conclusion' is on the causes and manifestations of James's chiasticism rather than on his own critical response to the literary works shaped by it. But he does express the view, which I would endorse, that the reader of James cannot look for compromise or synthesis between the various oppositions proposed: 'it is in the nature of chiasticism both to create the longing for them and at the same time to frustrate that same longing' (op. cit., p. 192).

2

Stephen Crane's *The Red Badge of Courage*: The Novella as 'Moving Box'

by A. ROBERT LEE

1

One of the most enduring memories of my literary life is the sensation produced by the appearance in 1895 of Crane's *Red Badge of Courage* in a small volume belonging to Mr. Heinemann's Pioneer Series of Modern Fiction. . . . Crane's work detonated on the mild din . . . of our sensibilities with the impact and force of a twelve-inch shell charged with a very high explosive. Unexpected it fell amongst us; and its fall was followed by a great outcry.

Not of consternation, however. The energy of that projectile hurt nothing and no one (such was its good fortune), and delighted a good many. It delighted soldiers, men of letters, men in the street; it was welcomed by all lovers of personal expression as a genuine revelation, satisfying the curiosity of a world in which war and love have been the subjects of song and story ever since the beginning of articulate speech.

—Joseph Conrad, 'His War Book': A Preface to Stephen Crane's
The Red Badge of Courage (1925)[1]

There was no real literature of our Civil War, excepting the forgotten 'Miss Ravenall's Conversion' by J. W. De Forest, until Stephen Crane wrote 'The Red Badge of Courage.' Crane wrote it before he had seen any war. But he had read the contemporary accounts, had heard the old soldiers, they were not so old then,

30

talk, and above all he had seen Matthew Brady's wonderful photographs. Creating his story out of this material he wrote that great boy's dream of war that was to be truer to how war is than any war the boy who wrote it would ever live to see. It is one of the finest books of our literature because it is all as much of one piece as a great poem is.

—Ernest Hemingway, Introduction to *Men at War* (1942)[2]

Had he lived beyond his brief span of twenty-nine years (1871-1900) and found himself reading these tributes, Stephen Crane might have derived a quite especial satisfaction. It could hardly be said that *The Red Badge of Courage* had not in fact won immediate and widespread attention, both the newspaper serial and then the book which came out in 1895 under the imprint of D. Appleton & Company. Indeed, over time, Crane actually came to fear that his other principal writings—work like 'Maggie: A Girl of the Streets' (1893), key collections such as *The Open Boat and Other Stories* (1898) and the *Whilomville Stories* (1900), his voluminous war reportage, and the dark, acerbic poetry of *The Black Riders and Other Lines* (1895) and *War is Kind* (1899)—risked almost permanent eclipse. Yet he would surely have recognized that both Conrad and Hemingway spoke from credentials of no simple order, but rather as writers profoundly of a kind.

In Conrad he would no doubt have thought warmly of the friendship developed across several interludes in England during the 1890s and of a body of fiction whose mastery in depicting human beings caught at the edge he had been quick to learn from and value. Nor would he have failed to see in Hemingway not only a fellow American war writer and journalist but a stylist in his own unmistakable and resolute mould. For in common with both of them, and beyond all the different issues of his 'naturalism' as it was thought, or his controversial life and marriage with Cora Taylor, or even his legend as yet another literary figure cut short before his time by consumption, it is Crane as himself the maker and stylist who before all else establishes his claims to attention, and nowhere more decisively than in *The Red Badge of Courage*.[3]

Not that Conrad and Hemingway do not touch base with most of the terms of references to have emerged in discussion of Crane's classic novella. Conrad, for instance, rightly comments on its appearance as 'unexpected'. Who would have thought a 'war book' at once as he calls it 'so virile' yet 'so full of gentle sympathy' and in all 'a gem' even to have been in the offing? More particularly still, who would have anticipated a major new imagining of the American Civil War three decades on from the surrender of the Confederate forces at Appomattox and from the pen of a writer never previously within earshot of actual military combat? Conrad's implicit reference-back, too, in phrasing like 'war and love', to the *Aeneid* (and by implication the *Iliad* and the *Odyssey*) were hardly amiss. Behind the telling of *The Red Badge of Courage* lies for certain the memory of older, more ancestral battles, be they those of Virgil, Homer, or indeed the Old Testament.

Hemingway, too, hits the mark in crediting Crane with having dramatized a conflict which as it has often been noted might well have become America's 'unwritten war'.[4] Besides the De Forest novel he mentions, which truly did draw upon its author's battle experience, one can properly cite verse like Whitman's *Drum Taps* (1865) and Melville's *Battle Pieces* (1866), or the great war passages in the autobiography of Abraham Lincoln, Ulysses S. Grant, William T. Sherman and Alexander H. Stephens (all most memorably analysed by Edmund Wilson in his *Patriotic Gore* (1962)), or cryptic story-telling like Twain's 'The Private History of a Campaign that Failed' (1885) and Ambrose Bierce's 'An Occurrence at Owl Creek Bridge' and 'Parker Adderson, Philosopher', both of which were reprinted in his *Tales of Soldiers and Civilians* (1891). One can also look back through pop-culture classics like Margaret Mitchell's *Gone with the Wind*, both the best-seller of 1936 and the Clark Gable-Vivien Leigh screen extravaganza released by M.G.M. in 1939, or MacKinlay Kantor's epic of the Confederacy's infamous prisoner-of-war camp *Andersonville* (1955). But whether these or virtually any other literary Civil War piece, none has come within range of *The Red Badge of Courage*.

As far as American fiction goes, it would also be remiss not to re-emphasize how much the tradition of war writing actually owes Crane. In him, despite possible other starting-points in Cooper or Hawthorne or Melville, it has its essential fountain-head. In the first place, there has to be Hemingway himself, the Nick Adams stories for instance, or *A Farewell to Arms*

(1929), or *For Whom the Bell Tolls* (1940), or his own prolific battle-line newspaper and periodical work. Nor is it difficult to discern Crane's impress elsewhere, be it as a documentary story-teller or visionary. It amounts to a kind of stupendous literary debt which stretches from key World War I novels like John Dos Passos's *Three Soldiers* (1921) and e. e. cummings's *The Enormous Room* (1922), through to World War II in the form among others of Norman Mailer's *The Naked and the Dead* (1948) and James Jones's *From Here to Eternity* (1951), and on into a later body of absurdist or apocalyptic fiction by the likes of John Hawkes, Mailer again, Kurt Vonnegut, Joseph Heller or Thomas Berger. Where Crane likely found his prime source in the Battle of Chancellorsville, his successors have turned to the Verdun trenches, the Japanese-held Pacific, Dresden, Italy, Korea and Vietnam. Yet as different as has been the locale, one outside America rather than within, or the idiom, rarely in Crane's own phrase has 'the sweep and fire' of men fighting under arms been better caught at essence.

The Red Badge of Courage has also found other contexts. If one boundary has been national, Crane not only as a classic American war writer but in company with William Dean Howells, Frank Norris, Theodore Dreiser and others as a classic American turn-of-the-century realist, another has been European. He has been likened to the English Great War poets, a Wilfred Owen or Isaac Rosenberg, though debate has swung about as to whether his is a vision of pity or of irony or even of celebration. A still bolder European direction is to be found in his own celebrated letter to John Northern Hilliard in which he basks in the praise accorded him by no lesser a dignitary than an English cabinet minister:

> I have only one pride—and may it be forgiven me. This single pride is that the English edition of 'The Red Badge' has been received with praise by the English reviewers. Mr. George Wyndham, Under Secretary for War in the British Government, says, in an essay, that the book challenges comparison with the most vivid scenes of Tolstoi's 'War and Peace' or of Zola's 'Downfall'; and the big reviews here praise it for just what I intended it to be, a psychological portrait of fear.[5]

Tolstoy and Zola as standards of comparison understandably aroused his pride, lofty world company indeed for a writer who goes on to allege that his aim amounts to no more than 'a slice of life', though one free of 'preaching' and 'moral lesson'. Little wonder that those with an untroubled confidence in categories like 'realism' and 'naturalism' have been quick to situate him in their camp.

The other great affinity which seems positively insisted upon in his work is with painting, Crane as a writer of acute visual and picturely accomplishment. His play of colours, of hues and shadings, signify that consciously or not he wrote as a literary impressionist, the imaginative fellow traveller of Monet and Pisarro, Renoir and Degas and Cézanne, and as tellingly as any, of his fellow countrymen Thomas Eakins of Philadelphia and the great Civil War photographer Mathew B. Brady, the latter rightly invoked by Hemingway as an inescapable force in Crane's fiction.[6] No doubt, too, one must take note of the illustrations Crane saw in *Battles and Leaders of the Civil War* (1884) and other popular accounts of the national conflict. But whatever the source, there can be few readers who do not emerge from Crane's novella without having been impressed by the energy of his pictorialism, sight (and sound) virtually absorbed into the prose upon the page. At every turn, too, in this connection, *The Red Badge of Courage* blends Henry Fleming's currents of feeling—from his nostalgic leave-taking from home to his boredom with military drilling to his rising panic and on to his many alternations of calm and shock—into the overall pictorialism. Colour, thereby, becomes a drama in itself, the text as a revolving prism of impressionistic reds, browns, blacks, greys, purples, whites and greens. But in giving full due to Crane's powers of visuality, it remains also to his credit that he neither overdoes these effects nor puts mere coloration ahead of his story's propulsion and dynamic.

Then, too, there has to be acknowledgement of the textual controversy which has arisen about *The Red Badge of Courage*. Here, the names of Fredson Bowers as the General Editor of *The University of Virginia Edition of the Works of Stephen Crane* (1969–75) and of the textual scholars Hershel Parker and Henry Binder assume prominence.[7] The latter advocate a 'reconstituted' *Red Badge* which puts back all the deletions (and much of the slang) originally to be found in the ms. first submitted to Appleton. The effect of this action may not be entirely as Binder originally titled his influential article of 1978 'The *Red Badge of Courage* Nobody Knows'—not at least if we compare in detail his eventual Avon text (1983) with that offered by Bowers and his associates in the University of Virginia *Works*—but it assuredly does make a difference. We meet a story whose irony comes over as still more uncompromising, in which Henry's eventual 'manhood' looks a thing more parodic than heroic, and in which the indictment of war takes on a still more evident commitment on Crane's part.

The present essay draws, to one degree or another, upon each of these perspectives. But it also suggests why of all story-telling forms the novella so suited Crane's purposes. In this, Conrad's emphasis upon 'a small volume', 'a gem', and Hemingway's upon *The Red Badge of Courage* as 'as much of one piece as a great poem is', despite the flawed versions of the text they were working from, can serve as points of departure. For there is about the work a virtual geometrical precision of design, a sense of story told to and within the strictest limits and co-ordinates. Crane, in a rightly acclaimed formulation, specifies his soldiery as enclosed 'in a moving box', men and army caught in two opposed cubes in which fear, injury, panic and death are likely at any time, as, to be sure, are selflessness and heroism. But the text itself, I suggest, can equally be thought 'a moving box', a means of enclosing the reader for a calculated amount of time in its own claustrophobia and pressure. The novella for Crane's purposes indeed could not be more apt, longer than the short story with its emphasis upon the single event and shorter than the novel with its capacity for the broad sweep and all the complication of extended height and depth. Henry's transformation from neophyte to veteran, and the ironies that attend upon it, Crane so fashions as to make us feel that we ourselves have been drawn into and locked precisely inside 'An Episode of the American Civil War', the book's greatly purposive sub-title.

2

Crane's opening of *The Red Badge of Courage* works to clear space for the reader, to enforce the transition from one reality to this, another:

> The cold passed reluctantly from the earth and the retiring fogs revealed an army stretched out on the hills, resting. As the

landscape changed from brown to green the army awakened and began to tremble with eagerness at the noise of rumors. It cast its eyes upon the roads which were growing from long troughs of liquid mud to proper thoroughfares. A river, amber-tinted in the shadow of its banks, purled at the army's feet and at night when the stream had become of a sorrowful blackness one could see, across, the red eye-like gleam of hostile camp-fires set in the low brows of distant hills.[8]

Without ado, cinematically we might now say, Crane shows us boundaries—latitudes and longitudes—actually coming into being. Night gives way to dawn, fogs lift, cold eases, brown yields to green, 'liquid mud' hardens into 'proper thoroughfares', a sleeping army awakens, silence gets replaced by 'the noise of rumors', and from its nocturnal 'sorrowful blackness' the river becomes 'amber-tinted'. Two encampments lie within sight of each other, that of the Union men on one hill, that of the Confederates on the hill facing. The latter's camp-fires overnight have glowed 'red' and 'eye-like', a kind of malignly fixed gaze.

Within these perameters the soldierly talk can indeed be thought to belong to men boxed by circumstance, by as yet unknown orders, by the hazards of weather and climate, and by the very battle-terrain itself. The talk, too, is of movement, change, maybe 't'morrah' and 'up th' river' as 'a certain tall soldier' says. But immediately he is countermanded by 'another private', who complains ' "I don't believe th' derned ol' army's ever goin' t' move" . . . "I've got ready t' move eight times in th' last two week an' we aint moved yit." ' A corporal, similarly, feels himself and his comrades to be 'in a sort of eternal camp'. The impulse towards movement is so checked, action and stasis built one against the other. The matter Crane then transfers to Henry Fleming himself, a conscript who believes himself as yet only 'a part of a vast blue demonstration', a victim of 'drill' and 'reviews'. Ironically he both craves the action which will transform him from novice to veteran yet endures the terror that he might 'run from a battle'. Not to fight, to fight, to run from the fight—these, too, come to focus in Jim Conklin's talk of past 'scrimmages'. If a soldier is to run, let him 'run like th' devil an' no mistake'; if not, 'stand an' fight'. Background and foreground are so joined, the prelude to action with the coming action.

The regiment waits on through yet another night, 'the youth' as Crane describes him 'clamoring at what he considered to be the intolerable slowness of the generals'. Orders arrive as if by unknown decree and 'a moment later' the regiment 'went swinging off into the darkness'. Other regiments march ahead and behind; in the banter 'whole brigades grinned in unison'; first 'black' and then 'purple' streaks mark the sky. And in the youth's interior musings there comes forth the key image of the book, or at least the one which bears most upon his traumatic fear of fleeing from battle:

> But he instantly saw that it would be impossible for him to escape from the regiment. It enclosed him. And there were iron laws of tradition and law on four sides. He was in a moving box.

And as the Army 'encloses' Henry, holds him in its 'will', so right across its twenty-five chapters *The Red Badge of Courage* 'encloses' the reader within its own language and effects, the story being told as though at one with the readership being created. Henry himself becomes a part of 'the line', 'the ranks', deviating only to step around the prophetically dead soldier whose boot soles have 'been worn to the thinnest of writing-paper'. Without pushing for too undue an emphasis upon self-reflexivity, it can be said that not only does Henry march at risk where other young soldiers have gone before but so his story in a sense has been written 'thin' before—by other authors writing about other battles in other places.

As the first battle for Henry comes up, Crane makes still further use of his box imagery. Having depicted Henry as first dug in, then promptly ordered to move, he refers to the youth's sight of 'horizontal flashes' ahead, the markers for 'the red animal, war, the blood-swollen god'. As he awaits his initiation, Henry thinks of the 'common personality' of an army, its 'single desire' for victory. The terms of his meditation could hardly be more to the point:

> He was at a task. He was like a carpenter who has made many boxes, making still another box, only there was furious haste in his movements. He, in his thoughts, was careering off in other places, even as the carpenter who as he works, whistles and thinks of his friend or his enemy, his home or a saloon. And these jolted dreams were never perfect to him afterward but remained a mass of blurred shapes.

Not only has Henry been 'boxed' by the army, by his own enlistment and training, he now chooses to accept and work inside his box. Only the onset of panic, blind intuitive panic, will cause him to seek extrication. Where to the one hand he has become 'not a man but a member', when he runs he will think of the enemy as 'machines of steel', of his fellows as 'machine-like idiots', and of himself as the 'proverbial chicken'. But 'escape' in fact proves an illusion. He runs only from one part of the box to another, ironically to be thought by his comrades honourably wounded in the line of duty rather than having been stunned by the random swing of a rifle. Henry's box, the box of war, in Crane's scheme permits no escape but merely variations within an overall control.

3

Of all the boxes-within-boxes delineated in the story, Crane offers none more chilling than Henry's encounter with the cadaver. As he flees for a moment the 'brittle blue line' and 'the rumble of death', he enters 'thick woods', a kind of natural stage-set which has been created to one side. Crane's terms are architectural. The copse he likens to 'a chapel', replete with 'green doors', 'a gentle brown carpet' and 'a religious half-light'. Henry has indeed found the 'dark and intricate place' he thinks of himself as having been seeking. The eddy of life that Crane refers us to could not be more bitterly ironic: the 'swishing saplings', the 'embraces of trees and vines', the 'rhythmical noises' of insects, the 'impudent head' of the woodpecker, the 'light-hearted wing' of a bird, the 'jovial squirrel', and even the 'small animal' which pounces upon 'a silver-gleaming fish'. If these can be thought the benign life-forms of the place, on crossing the inmost 'threshold' Henry comes upon a quite counter form:

> He was being looked at by a dead man who was seated with his back against a column-like tree. The corpse was dressed in a uniform that once had been blue but was now faded to a melancholy shade of green. The eyes, staring at the youth, had changed to the dull hue to be seen on the side of a dead fish. The mouth was opened. Its red had changed to an appalling yellow.

Over the grey skin of the face ran little ants. One was trundling some sort of a bundle across the upper lip.

The youth gave a shriek as he confronted the thing. He was, for moments, turned to stone before it. He remained staring into the liquid-looking eyes. The dead man and the living man exchanged a long look. . . .

At last, he burst the bonds which had fastened him to the spot and fled, unheeding the underbrush. He was pursued by a sight of the black ants swarming greedily upon the grey face and venturing horribly near to the eyes. . . .

The trees about the portal of the chapel moved sighingly in a soft wind. A sad silence was upon the little, guarding edifice. . . .

He thought as he remembered the small animal capturing the fish and the greedy ants feeding upon the flesh of the dead soldier, that there was given another law which far-over-topped it—all life existing upon death, eating ravenously, stuffing itself with the hopes of the dead.

And nature's processes were obliged to hurry.

The horror of the encounter needs not to be insisted upon so sure is Crane's touch. The exchange of 'looks', the blue uniform fading into a melancholy green, the 'appalling' yellow of a once red mouth, and above all, the ants close to the dead soldier's eyes, all combine to make a portrait of that 'other law' which sets the living not only upon the living but even upon the dead. War as fought by men has its analogue in the scavenging wars of Nature. Not for Crane some Wordsworthian uplifting Nature, but one which simply operates to neutral rules, those of supply and demand. Henry leaves this 'box' to flee back to that of the larger one, that which 'was like the grinding of an immense and terrible machine to him'. Having, too, seen the image of death, he finds himself listening to a ditty which serves up its own cryptic commentary:

> 'Sing a song 'a vic'try
> A pocketful 'a bullets
> Five an' twenty dead men
> Baked in a—pie.'

'Baked', or 'boxed', Henry like his compeers has only an enclosed amount of space as a soldier in which to move. Crane ensures that we, matchingly, are drawn into that enclosure and made to experience its domination.

4

The return to 'the place of fighting' and Henry's last mock-glorious apotheosis as a soldier begins with his witness of Jim Conklin's death and ends in his taking hold of the regimental flag. Conklin's death-dance, a doomed pirouette under the 'red sun', transfers itself to Henry's own physical sensations, not unlike the 'spasm' in Melville's *Billy Budd* which passes from the young Foretopman to Captain Vere as the former is hanged from the yard-arm aboard the *Bellipotent*. Henry has no choice but to take into himself the grotesque ceremony of Conklin's transition from life to death. He both witnesses and inwardly re-enacts this descent from movement into stasis, from motion into motionlessness. But first he thinks longingly of his own wish for 'a red badge', a wound, to match that of Jim Conklin. He then stands transfixed by Conklin's 'running' into a nearby clearing, himself the veteran of having 'run' and just as absurdly. He experiences a matching 'strangeness' in his own momentarily static body as Conklin hits the ground 'in the manner of a falling tree'. His last sight is of Conklin's death's-head grin, mouth open and teeth clenched 'in a laugh'. Crane's effects are both energetically particular and symptomatic of the novella at large: a veteran dying inside the box watched by his successor, one 'enclosed' soldier watched by another equally 'enclosed'.

He has Henry cling, nonetheless, to the illusion that he is in possession of a separate, unique existence, one somehow exempt from 'universal laws' and 'system'. Henry also looks to make good on his self-estimation as a Cain branded by 'the marks of his flight'; he has become a newly willing member of 'the mighty blue machine' who will find his nemesis as a *miles gloriosus*. But no sooner has he so resolved than the box closes in on him once again as he meets Union soldiers heading back from a skirmish with the enemy:

> Presently, men were running hither and thither, in all ways. The artillery booming, forward, rearward, and on the flanks made jumble of ideas of direction. Landmarks had vanished into the gathered gloom. The youth began to imagine he had gotten

into the centre of the tremendous quarrel and he could perceive
no way out of it. From the mouths of the fleeing men came a
thousand wild questions but no one made answers.

Fleming indeed knows only *huis clos*, 'the tremendous quarrel'
and 'no way out of it'.

Even as he joins up with his own regiment, 'Th' 304th
N'York', he has no clear or coherent sense of 'direction'.
Crane's imagery again speaks of a boxed-in arena of death:
'The forest seemed a vast hive of men buzzing about in frantic
circles. . . .' Hived is precisely what Henry and his fellows are,
insect men driven by forces they can neither understand nor
control. Even the talk about the enemy contains its own
familiar image: ' "All th' officers say we've got th' rebs in
a pretty tight box." ' Returned to his regiment Henry may
be, re-linked with his friend Wilson, ironically honoured for
his 'wound', but he has done no more than join precisely his
own side's 'box'. He sleeps as if 'he had been asleep for a
thousand years', the sleep of the dead. And in waking, he sees
in what also has become a familiar image the 'box' as nothing
less than a fantastical morgue, an Army 'charnel house'. The
terms of reference are appropriately those of immuration and
burial:

> About him, were the rows and groups of men that he had
> dimly seen the previous night. They were getting a last draught
> of sleep before the awakening. The gaunt, care-worn faces and
> dusty figures were made plain by this quaint light at the dawning
> but it dressed the skin of the men in corpse-like hues and made
> the tangled limbs appear pulseless and dead. The youth started
> up with a little cry when his eyes first swept over this motionless
> mass of men, thick-spread upon the ground, pallid and in strange
> postures. His disordered mind interpreted the hall of the forest
> as a charnel place. He believed for an instant that he was in the
> house of the dead and he did not dare to move lest these corpses
> start up, squalling and squarking.

Hieronymus Bosch might have found his text here, soldierly
death seen in terms of a baroque interment.

Onwards Henry and the others march 'in a spread column'.
The talk again bespeaks a will to action and movement. Crane,
however, has one of Henry's youthful companions complain as

41

follows, the vernacular talk of a soldier damned at once by inaction and action:

> 'Good Gawd,' . . . 'we're allus bein' chased around like rats. It makes me sick. Nobody seems ti know where we go ner why we go. We jest git fired around from piller t' post an' git licked here an' licked there an' nobody knows what it's done fer. It makes a man feel like a damn' kitten in a bag. . . .'

A kitten 'bagged' adds another term to the text's lexicon of enclosure, alongside 'boxed' and 'baked'. As they get ready for the next engagement, too, Henry's companions are said to stand 'as men tied to stakes', fixity in the face of movement. Crane, here as elsewhere, draws us into this alternating set of 'pulses', one contraflow set against the other, but all situated within the enframing box. The action inscribed by the text blends into, and becomes at one with, the text itself.

Henry accedes to the regiment's 'forward movement', fighting 'like a pagan' and in despite of the 'shaggy man' who says to him ' "We'll git swallered." ' He sees only 'the land in front of him' while behind lies 'a coherent trail of bodies'. He lurches onwards with the others, in Crane's image, 'involved like a cart involved in mud and muddle', the regiment as a whole a 'scurrying mass'. The regiment temporarily falls back 'to the stolid trees', and Henry and Wilson tussle for who will carry the flag. Henry wins, takes the flag upon himself, and serves as the spur to the regiment which has become 'a machine run-down'. Crane's irony sharpens to a fine point: the would-be escapee from the box has become the very emblem-bearer of its control. The focus pulls back slightly again to enclose us in company with the soldiers in its inescapability:

> The way seemed eternal. In the clouded haze, men became panic-stricken with the thought that the regiment had lost its path and was proceeding in a perilous direction. Once, the men who headed the wild procession turned and came pushing back against their comrades screaming that they were being fired upon from points which they had considered to be toward their own lines. At this cry, a hysterical fear and dismay beset the troops. A soldier who heretofore had been ambitious to make the regiment into a wise little band that would proceed calmly amid the huge-appearing difficulties, suddenly sank down and buried his face in his arms

with an air of bowing to a doom. From another, a shrill lamenta-
tion rang out filled with profane allusions to a general. Men ran
hither and thither seeking with their eyes, roads of escape. With
serene regularity as if controlled by a schedule, bullets buffed
into men.

'Roads of escape', like 'no way out of it', offers the perfect gloss.
To become 'men' the troops must fight 'in the manner of a pair
of boxers', two 'bodies of soldiers' whose 'fast, angry firings'
compel them to a fixed antagonism. Both in terms of space and
time they are locked one into the other, 'scheduled' bullets
dropping them 'serenely' into death. They hear, too, other
engagements in the distance, other lines of conflict taking place
within the box. And through it all 'the youth' keeps 'the bright
colors to the front', the moving box's forward herald and
standard-bearer. The regiment becomes 'a flying regiment', its
different 'sides' and 'walls' geometrically welded into a whole.
No matter that as a regiment it has 'bled extravagantly', nor
that Henry has foresworn all thoughts of escaping the 'entrap-
ment' he associates with the four captured Confederate soldiers.
The box has claimed him, and for the moment us, wholly.

5

'The regiment marched until it had joined its fellows.' So,
in the novella's last chapter, Crane reminds that this one box
belongs inside a succession of others. The regiment fits inside
'the brigade', and the brigade inside the Union army as a whole.
'Dust-covered' troops reassemble 'in column' and 'parallel to
the enemy's lines', yet once again a squared configuration in
place to continue the conflict. Henry and his companion Wilson,
however, have lost all sight of the boundaries. They bathe in
'the gilded images of memory' as to their first 'successful' battle.
Henry feels a 'coronation' in the lieutenant's praise that he has
fought like 'a wildcat'. Even the 'shoutings in his brain' about
his temptation to run and his possible 'shame' are silenced.
He regards himself as a triumphant figure, once 'a novice who
did not understand' but now the actual beneficiary of 'fate'.
Crane's cryptic summary runs: 'it was suddenly clear to him
that he had been wrong not to kiss the knife and bow to the
cudgel.' A would-be fleer from the box, he has become its most

settled resident, a promoter of its supposed manhood-conferring powers. To argue the claims of the box, to embrace and proclaim them, in Crane's angling suggests an even more fatal form of enclosure.

What Henry has ceased to see, but Crane makes us see, is the price of this new stage of self-enboxment. Manhood has come to mean acceptance of a militarized universe, the squared and paired-off divisions of war. Henry experiences in this acceptance 'sudden flashes of joy', 'a quiet manhood', a 'soul changed'. Crane also returns us to where we began, a picturing 'frame' for 'the red sickness of battle', one whose meanings for Henry have to do only with the necessary restoration before more battling, more further deeds of glory:

> It rained. The procession of weary soldiers became a bedraggled train, despondent and muttering, marching with churning effort, in a trough of liquid brown mud under a low, wretched sky. Yet the youth smiled, for he saw that the world was a world for him though many discovered it to be made of oaths and walking-sticks. He had rid himself of the red sickness of battle. The sultry night-mare was in the past. He had been an animal blistered and sweating in the heat and pain of war. He turned now with a lover's thirst, to images of tranquil skies, fresh meadows, cool brooks; an existence of soft and eternal peace.

Crane's frame for his story, as it were, lowers and closes in upon Henry, the 'low wretched sky' at one with the ground-level 'liquid brown mud'. This reducing scale, the nearness with which Nature is focused, the literal touching of heaven and earth, all again confirm Crane's sureness in directing parts into the whole, details into form. That form, of course, is for him the novella, deployed as purposefully as can be to his needs of proportion, height and depth. Crane matches his story-telling to his story as if instinctively, the intensity and duration of his young soldier's rite of passage pressed into exact narrative mould.

6

'In a moving box': the phrase works in every way to the two principal ends above. On the one hand it captures Henry's experience in having signed up with and having been absorbed into the regiment, and then his subsequent demarch into battle.

Equally, and correspondingly, it underlines how *The Red Badge of Courage* operates as itself a kind of fictional 'box' which encloses the reader within its own precisely drawn and regulated boundaries. In both respects, too, we can again turn to observations made by Crane's fellow novelists. The first returns us to Conrad, who praised Crane not only for a powerful war story (he calls Henry 'the symbol of all untried men') but for *The Red Badge* as a vindication of story-telling craft:

> But as to 'masterpiece', there is no doubt that *The Red Badge of Courage* is that, if only because of the marvellous accord of the vivid impressionistic description of action on that woodland battlefield, and the imaged style of analysis of emotions in the inward moral struggle going on in the breast of one individual—the young soldier of the book, the protagonist of the monodrama presented to us in an endless succession of graphic and coloured phrases.[9]

Conrad's use of terms like 'the marvellous accord' and 'monodrama', albeit in their own way, again speak directly to the qualities of concentration which make Crane's novella so right in its choice of form.

A similar set of judgements is to be found in Ralph Ellison's notable Introduction to his 1960 selection of Crane short stories.[10] Having first praised Crane's 'courage' in resisting the 'noisy clamor' of late nineteenth-century American war-fever and jingoism, he goes on to speak of Crane's work as 'a triumph of art'. In part, this has to do with its 'realistic poetry'; even more, it has to do with its success as a tale 'unerringly' told. For Ellison, as for other readers, *The Red Badge of Courage* achieves that rare thing, the unmistakable integration of theme—'an episode of the American Civil War' and the war and peace within the human breast—and of story-telling design.[11] Both dimensions coalesce perfectly in the phrase 'in a moving box', Crane's very marker for the workings of his landmark novella.

NOTES

1. Republished in Joseph Conrad, *Last Essays* (London and New York: J. M. Dent & Sons, 1926).
2. Ernest Hemingway, *Men at War: The Best War Stories of All Time* (New York: Crown Publishers, 1942).
3. The standard Crane biographies are: Thomas Beer, *Stephen Crane: A Study in American Letters* (New York: Alfred A. Knopf, 1923); John Berryman, *Stephen Crane*, American Men of Letters Series (New York: William Sloane Associates, 1950); Eric Solomon, *Stephen Crane in England: A Portrait of the Artist* (Columbus, Ohio: Ohio State University Press, 1964); R. W. Stallman, *Stephen Crane: A Biography* (New York: George Braziller Inc., 1968); and Edwin H. Cady's revised Twayne's United States Authors Series volume, *Stephen Crane* (Boston: G.K. Hall & Co., 1962, 1980). I have also benefited from Theodore L. Gross and Stanley Wertheim, *Hawthorne, Melville, Stephen Crane: A Critical Bibliography* (New York and London: Collier-Macmillan Ltd., The Free Press, 1971).
4. See, especially, Daniel Aaron, *The Unwritten War: American Writers and the Civil War* (New York: Alfred A. Knopf, 1973).
5. This celebrated letter was written to John Northern Hilliard in January 1896. See R. W. Stallman and Lillian Gilkes (eds.), *Stephen Crane's Letters* (New York: New York University Press, 1960), pp. 31–2. George Wyndham's original review appeared as 'A Remarkable Book' in the *New Review*, XIV (January 1896), 30–40.
6. On the connection with Eakins, see Michael Fried, *Realism, Writing, Disfiguration: On Thomas Eakins and Stephen Crane* (Chicago: University of Chicago Press, 1987).
7. The sequence of relevant scholarship is as follows: Fredson Bowers (ed.), *The University of Virginia Edition of the Works of Stephen Crane* (Charlottesville: University Press of Virginia, 1969–75); Henry Binder, 'The *Red Badge of Courage* Nobody Knows', *Studies in the Novel*, 10 (1978), 9–47; Henry Binder (ed.), *The Red Badge of Courage: An Episode of the American Civil War* (New York: W. W. Norton, 1982; and New York: Avon Books, 1983); and Hershel Parker, 'Getting Used to the "Original Form" of *The Red Badge of Courage*' in Lee Clark Mitchell (ed.), *New Essays on 'The Red Badge of Courage'* (Cambridge: Cambridge University Press, 1986), pp. 25–47.
8. All quotations are from the Avon edition of the text (New York: Avon Books, 1983).
9. *Last Essays*, op. cit.
10. Ralph Ellison, Introduction to *The Red Badge of Courage and Four Great Stories by Stephen Crane* (New York: Dell Publishing Co., 1960).
11. Crane scholarship has, predictably, been prolific. But I want to acknowledge, especially, the following: James T. Cox, 'The Imagery of "The Badge of Courage" ', *Modern Fiction Studies*, V (Autumn 1959), 209–19; Mordecai Marcus, 'The Unity of *The Red Badge of Courage*' in Richard Lettis *et al.* (eds.), *The Red Badge of Courage: Text and Criticism* (New York:

Harcourt, Brace & Co., 1960), pp. 189-95; Edwin H. Cady, *Stephen Crane* (1962, 1980), op. cit.; Warner Berthoff, *The Ferment of Realism: American Literature 1884–1919* (New York and London: Collier-Macmillan Ltd., The Free Press, 1965); Jay Martin, *Harvests of Change: American Literature 1865–1914* (Englewood Cliffs, New Jersey: Prentice-Hall, 1967); Donald B. Gibson, *The Fiction of Stephen Crane* (Carbondale, Illinois: Southern Illinois University Press, 1968); and Lee Clark Mitchell (ed.), *New Essays on 'The Red Badge of Courage'* (1986), op. cit.

3

Kate Chopin's *The Awakening:* 'Casting Aside that Fictitious Self'

by DOROTHY GOLDMAN

Is it significant that in the early years of Kate Chopin's rediscovery, sexual interpretations of *The Awakening* came most frequently from men? One thinks of Larzer Ziff: '*The Awakening* was the most important piece of fiction about the sexual life of a woman written to date in America.' Or Kenneth Elbe: 'Quite frankly, the book is about sex. Not only is it about sex, but the very texture of the writing is sensuous, if not sensual, from the first to the last.'[1] More recently women critics have been less astonished by the discovery of female sexuality and have identified another, equally complex, subject. Paula A. Treichler, for example, writes, 'We may have believed that *The Awakening* has been building towards Edna's sexual fulfilment, but we are wrong . . . both body and spirit are awakening towards some final end, and this is not it', and Barbara C. Ewell describes Edna's recognition of her sexuality as 'a critical *prelude* to consciousness'.[2] The book may be suffused with passion and the language almost unremittingly sensual, but sexuality is *not* its central concern; it is only the catalyst to self-knowledge, the medium through which Edna Pontellier discovers her identity.

Initially, identity may seem an ambitious concept to tackle within the necessarily limited scope of the novella: that Kate

Chopin objectifies this nebulous and protean subject in a psychologically detailed portrait of a woman whose self-discovery inevitably leads to self-destruction makes her chosen form even more unlikely. The following analysis of *The Awakening* suggests that Chopin's achievement relies upon the additional functions consistently performed by the story's externals in charting Edna Pontellier's progress to self-understanding; characters, plot, language, imagery, narrator—all illumine the changes that are taking place in her soul and, as they are pared away, expose the innate nature of her predicament. Chopin uses other characters, for example, as rôle models which the heroine experiments with but finally rejects; even the narrator, whose language initially mimics the heroine's confused and inarticulate understanding of the process of self-realization, must finally be abandoned by her. This uncertain narrative stance is compounded by the relationship of plot and imagery which are not kept separate but partially conflated to allow of mutual influence and interpretation. Finally Edna Pontellier will stand alone with her memories: the process of discovery will not be easy.

Who does she discover herself to be and why does it ultimately lead to her death?

> Edna felt as if she were being borne away from some anchorage which had held her fast, whose chains had been loosening—had snapped the night before when the mystic spirit was abroad, leaving her free to drift whithersoever she chose to set her sails.[3]

The 'night before' Edna had learnt to swim—a metaphor for her awakened sexuality, a metaphor which Kate Chopin here extends: no longer merely a swimmer, Edna is now a boat that has snapped its chains. Chopin's prose is never simple, however, and the increased power suggested by 'snapped' is negated by the impotence of 'being borne away', and these contradictions are further compounded when Edna is described as being *'free to drift* whithersoever she *chose to set her sails'* (my emphasis). The relationship between drift and choice in Edna Pontellier's journey of self-discovery is complex; the apparent contradictions will ultimately be seen to converge.

Elements of choice seem to be clearly signalled in the plot.

The individual steps of Edna's rebellion against a socially-imposed identity are clearly marked: she can leave her husband's house, and does so; she can take a lover, and does so. But there is a further series of subtextual options available to her which she flirts with; at Grand Isle they are represented by the lady in black and the lovers. In this initial stage of her awakening she has 'two alternatives—renunciation and fulfillment—as symbolized by the lady in black and the young lovers respectively'.[4] Zlotnick's interpretation can be further particularized: the lady in black is seen 'telling her beads' (4), 'reading her morning devotions' (17), 'with her Sunday prayer book, velvet and gold-clasped, and her Sunday silver beads' (33) and 'counting her beads for the third time' (34). Edna briefly tries this specifically religious option, but a

> feeling of oppression and drowsiness overcame [her] during the service. Her head began to ache, and the lights on the altar swayed before her eyes. . . . [H]er one thought was to quit the stifling atmosphere of the church and reach the open air. (36)

When the lady in black is asked what has affected Edna, she does not reply but keeps 'her eyes fastened upon the pages of her velvet prayer-book' (36). Religion will not compensate Edna for the loss of love, and she and the lady in black have nothing to say to each other, never speak.

The proximity of the appearances of the lovers to those of the lady in black points to their relationship as alternatives. The lovers are seen 'leaning towards each other' (22), 'exchanging . . . hearts' yearnings . . . vows and sighs' (17, 20); but this time it is Robert who destroys the option which they represent. He 'walked between them, whether with malicious or mischievous intent was not wholly clear, even to himself' (27). Back in New Orleans Edna still wishes to adopt this identity, seeking a romantic future with Robert rather than the loveless pleasure which Arobin offers; but on his return from Mexico Robert rejects it in reality as firmly as he did figuratively on Grand Isle.

These are not Edna's only 'horizons of experience'.[5] At Grand Isle she had listened to Mademoiselle Reisz practise a piece which she imagines is called 'Solitude'.

> When she heard it there came before her imagination the figure of a man standing beside a desolate rock on the seashore. He was

naked. His attitude was one of hopeless resignation as he looked toward a distant bird winging its flight away from him. (26–7)

It is not fanciful to believe that this figure constitutes a third variant on Edna's position, for she also experiments with identity as a man. Not only does she take her sexual pleasure in the manner traditionally associated with men, but there were 'few track men . . . [who] knew the race horse as well as Edna, . . . certainly none who knew it better' (74). She drinks 'liquor from the glass as a man would have done' (79). She imitates her husband who had 'instructed' her to dismiss Robert if he became boring, by later 'commanding his presence' (33). Like her husband she pays a short visit to her children in the country and remembers them with a gift:

> She stopped at a confectioner's and ordered a huge box of bonbons for the children in Iberville. She slipped a card in the box, on which she scribbled a tender message and sent an abundance of kisses. (81–2)

As an absentee parent Edna actually outperforms her husband; although Mr. Pontellier had 'promised to bring [the children] back bonbons and peanuts' (5), he forgot.

A second contrasted pair of identities which Edna might adopt comes to the fore on her return to New Orleans. 'In the summer of her awakening, she has two female foils who incarnate the extremes of possibility for her.'[6] The first, representing the very opposite of life as a man, is Madame Ratignolle. Their friendship, whose origins are described as sensuously as the relationship between Edna and Robert, begins on the beach at Grand Isle where the 'Pontellier and Ratignolle compartments adjoined one another under the same roof' (16). What Madame Ratignolle has to offer is the rôle of 'mother-woman'. Such women

> seemed to prevail that summer at Grand Isle. It was easy to know them, fluttering about with extended, protecting wings when any harm, real or imaginary, threatened their precious brood. They were women who idolized their children, worshiped their husbands, and esteemed it a holy privilege to efface themselves as individuals and grow wings as ministering angels. (10)

Madame Ratignolle, who has a 'more feminine and matronly figure' (16) than Edna, is not only pregnant but pictured with two of her children clinging to her skirts and the third carried 'in her own fond, encircling arms' (14). Edna tries out this rôle, albeit briefly, when, 'under Madame Ratignolle's directions' (10), she makes baby-garments; but she rebels against its inevitable consequences. It is at Madame Ratignolle's *accouchement* that she experiences her 'flaming, outspoken revolt against the ways of Nature' (109).

If the self-effacing Madame Ratignolle combines sensuousness and maternity, Edna's alternate model, the 'self-assertive' (26) Mademoiselle Reisz, combines passion and artistry. Once in New Orleans Edna seeks her out when she has to be sought and begged to visit by Madame Ratignolle. She makes a concerted effort to emulate the pianist, letting her housekeeping standards drop, living alone and painting. Mademoiselle Reisz warns her of the dangers inherent in adopting the rôle of artistic rebel:

> The bird that would soar above the level plain of tradition and prejudice must have strong wings. It is a sad spectacle to see the weaklings bruised, exhausted, fluttering back to earth. (82)

Furthermore in her music she predicts the disaster which will ensue if Edna assumes such an identity—music is second only to the sea as a symbol of sexual passion in *The Awakening* and almost as destructive. When Edna reads Robert's first letter Mademoiselle Reisz plays to her:

> Gradually and imperceptibly the interlude melted into the soft opening minor chords of the Chopin Impromptu. . . . [She] glided from the Chopin into the quivering love-notes of Isolde's song, and back again to the Impromptu with its soulful and poignant longing.
>
> The shadows deepened in the little room. The music grew strange and fantastic—turbulent, insistent, plaintive and soft with entreaty. The shadows grew deeper. The music filled the room. It floated out upon the night, over the housetops, the crescent of the river, losing itself in the silence of the upper air. (64)

The danger to Edna is marked in Mademoiselle Reisz's choice of Wagner's *Liebestod*, its partial amalgamation into water imagery and in the darkening shadows. When Edna leaves, Mademoiselle Reisz warns her: ' "Be careful; the stairs and landings are dark; don't stumble" ' (64). Just before Edna's death the warning about the need for strong wings, the music—'insistent, plaintive and soft with entreaty'—and Edna's interpretation of 'Solitude' fuse and are transposed from metaphor into personal experience:

> The voice of the sea is seductive, never ceasing, whispering, clamoring, murmuring, inviting the soul to wander in abysses of solitude. All along the white beach, up and down, there was no living thing in sight. A bird with a broken wing was beating the air above, reeling, fluttering, circling disabled down, down to the water. . . . [F]or the first time in her life [Edna] stood naked in the open air. (113)[7]

Similar metaphorical formations embody the options and constraints which surround Edna. Typical are the references to birds—caged and free—which, from the opening lines of *The Awakening*, perform a significant defining function. The trilingual parrot's cry of ' "*Allez vous-en!*" ' may stand as a warning to women at the book's very outset, but more significant is the disparaging connection between women and birds which Mr. Pontellier initiates; he identifies both the parrot and the mocking-bird as 'the property of Madame Lebrun' (3) and subsequently looks at his wife 'as one looks at a valuable piece of personal property' (4).[8] The mocking-bird, though outdoors, is in a cage and no more free than the caged parrot, who in speaking attempts to conform to the world of its captors. The similarity in their situations is analogous to Edna's circumstances before and after she leaves her husband's house. She has also remained within the social sphere of her 'captors': even when she sets up house by herself she goes only 'around the block' (82) and significantly to a 'pigeon-house'. Describing the mother-women Chopin uses the words 'fluttering . . . protecting wings . . . brood . . . grow wings as ministering angels' (see p. 51 above). The fusion of angelic imagery with that of domesticated fowls would constitute a clearly derogatory comment on the rôle of 'the angel in the house', even if it stood alone; as part of a chain of imagery which equates domestic fowl with property, the effect is even more scornful. It is within this context that we must understand the references to flight possible for wild birds.

At the dinner party given for her father and Dr. Mandelet,

Edna Pontellier tells a story which is as self-revealing as those of her guests. Mr. Pontellier, as host, tells 'amusing plantation experiences'; Edna's father (who 'perhaps unaware that he had coerced his own wife into her grave' will recommend ' "Authority [and] coercion" ' ((71) to Léonce Pontellier in his dealings with Edna) tells a story of his war experiences; the doctor (who understands Edna's restlessness but hopes for a conventionally happy outcome) tells

> the old, ever new and curious story of the waning of a woman's love, seeking strange, new channels, only to return to its legitimate source after days of fierce unrest.

Rejecting this hope ('The story did not seem especially to impress Edna'), she tells the tale of a woman

> who paddled away with her lover one night in a pirogue and never came back. . . . It was a pure invention. . . . Perhaps it was a dream she had had. But every glowing word seemed real to those who listened. They could feel the hot breath of the Southern night; they could hear . . . the beating of birds' wings, rising startled from among the reeds in the salt-water pools. (70)

What they are hearing is a fantasy on the day Edna and Robert sailed to *Chênière Caminada*, but one in which through the imagery of flight Edna now asserts her power to escape. As Mlle. Reisz had feared, however, her wings are not strong enough to let her rise, and the 'disabled' bird she sees just before her death with its 'broken wing . . . beating the air' flutters 'down, down' (113) into the sea.

This movement from metaphorical birds to actual birds which have a metaphorical function is typical of *The Awakening*, a work characterized by a disorienting shift between events and the metaphorical language which describes them.[9] Edna's reworking of the trip to *Chênière Caminada* has a textual justification. At the end of the visit, when she and Robert step

> into Tonie's boat, with the red lateen sail, misty spirit forms were prowling in the shadows and among the reeds, and upon the water were phantom ships, speeding to cover. (39–40)

Are we to understand these spirits and ships as figments of Edna's imagination, stimulated by Mme. Antoine's stories? Are they part of the figurative language of the novella, where 'a spirit that . . . rises up from the Gulf' (30) represents Edna's sexuality and where Edna herself is imaged as a boat? Or are they vouchsafed an actual existence? No wonder the provenance of Edna's story is confused:

> Madame Antoine had *related* it to her. That . . . was an *invention.* Perhaps it was a *dream* she had had. . . . The champagne was cold, and its subtle fumes played fantastic tricks with Edna's *memory* that night. (70–1: my emphases)

The unreliable nature of story-telling, Edna's dreams and her memory reflect different orders of awareness present throughout the book; each must be considered if we are to understand what elements go to make up Edna Pontellier and who she comes to understand herself to be.

It has generally been agreed that Chopin 'combines *a detached tone* with a sensuous prose that strongly enforces the point of Edna's awakening' and that 'her *implicit* approval is stated, through metaphor, on almost every page'; that while Chopin 'obviously sympathize[s] with Mrs. Pontellier' she '*makes no explicit comment* on Edna Pontellier's actions. . . . *neither approves nor condemns, but maintains an aesthetic distance* throughout, relying upon the recurring patterns of imagery to convey her meaning.'[10] This is not, however, true. Though the author introduces the heroine objectively—describing her through Mr. Pontellier's eyes—the amorphous narrative stance includes occasions when the narrator signifies her presence and identifies herself with Edna's attitudes. When Mme. Ratignolle is introduced it is as one of the mother-women, 'the fair lady of *our* dreams' (10); the warm relationship which she and Edna share is more than companionship—'Who can tell what metals the gods use in forging the subtle bond which *we* call sympathy, which *we* might as well call love' (15). More significantly, Edna's marriage requires submission and 'obedience to his compelling wishes . . . unthinkingly, as *we* walk, move, sit, stand, go through the daily treadmill of the life which has been portioned to *us*' (32). Describing the chaos in Edna's soul as she begins to discover who she is, the narrator comments 'How few of *us* ever emerge from such beginning! How many souls perish in its tumult!' (15); writing of the changes in Edna's character she says that Mr. Pontellier 'could not see that she was becoming herself and daily casting aside that fictitious self which *we* assume like a garment with which to appear before the world' (57: my emphases throughout).

This supportive (and implicitly female) narrator contributes to the textual ambiguity which surrounds the portrait of Edna Pontellier—there frequently appears to be no boundary between her and her subject. The quite specifically ambiguous uses of the words 'perhaps' show that often the narrator is no more certain of the truth about Edna than the heroine herself. Edna's love for the sad-eyed cavalry officer occurred during her childhood—'perhaps it was when she traversed the ocean of waving grass' (18). When Mlle. Reisz plays to the company at Grand Isle, Edna responds passionately: 'Perhaps it was the first time she was ready, perhaps the first time her being was tempered to take an impress of the abiding truth' (27). 'Perhaps' the fantasy on the visit to *Chênière Caminada* was a dream, 'perhaps' her father was 'unaware that he had coerced his own wife into her grave' (71). It is not possible to understand these instances as indicating transitions into the consciousness of the character.[11] The uncertainty resides within the influential but elusive narrator—and is further compounded in unsettling verbal jokes. When, for example, Edna received Mr. Pontellier's hamper her friends 'declared that Mr. Pontellier was the best husband in the world. Mrs. Pontellier was forced to admit that she knew of none better' (9). It is not possible to determine whether we are to understand this ironically—nor whether the possible irony reflects the narrator's opinion or is intended by Edna herself.

Perhaps the narrator regards the truth as impenetrable, or, if known, as inexpressible. The book abounds in phrases which signal the impossibility of understanding or communication. Edna is introduced as being ' "burnt beyond recognition" ' (4). The parrot speaks 'a language which nobody understood' (3) and Edna and Mme. Ratignolle 'did not appear to understand each other or to be talking the same language' (48). Edna suffers an 'indescribable oppression' (8). 'There are no words to describe' Adèle Ratignolle (10); the way she and Edna escape Robert is 'unaccountable' (15), as is Edna's satisfaction at the lukewarm nature of her love for her husband. Robert cannot express his intuitive understanding of Edna's emotions: 'He could not explain; he could not tell her that he had penetrated her mood and understood. He said nothing' (30). Victor's interview with Edna begins when he shouts at his servant; his abuse 'owing to its rapidity and incoherence, was all but incomprehensible' (59). Soon he begins to speak of his escapades—'Of course, he couldn't think of telling Mrs. Pontellier all about it, she being a woman and not comprehending such things' (60). Like the narrator, when Edna does try to express herself she cannot. 'She felt that her speech was voicing the incoherency of her thoughts and stopped abruptly. . . . "Oh! I don't know what I'm saying, Doctor" ' (109–10).

Edna Pontellier's final act of self-identification and self-knowledge will occur when she cuts herself off from this uncertain narrator, much as she had earlier discarded her fictional alternate identities. It is a feat which is only fully achieved in the last chapter—a chapter in which 'the unreliable nature of story telling' is rejected in favour of a narrative divided between objective and subjective prose. The former resides in the scenes between Victor and Mariequita and Edna's preparations for suicide: the latter in an increasingly direct presentation of her meditations, memories and sensations. Treichler suggests that

> The Awakening charts Edna Pontellier's growing mastery of the first person singular, and that when this 'I' has been created, the book has successfully completed its mission and comes to an end.[12]

'Dream' and 'memory' have their part to play in Edna's ability progressively to cut herself free from the narrator and become the first person singular.

Treichler points out that in describing Edna and her inner life Chopin gives importance to abstract nouns and the passive voice, so that Edna appears 'the silent, baffled receptacle for feelings that fill her mindlessly'.[13] More specifically, Wolff notes that

> The words which recur most frequently to describe [Edna] are words like melting, drifting, misty, dreaming, shadowy. She is not willing (perhaps not able) to define her position in the world.[14]

An extension of Wolff's list shows how this vocabulary group characteristically describes Edna's inward state, not her outward behaviour: 'inward maze of contemplation' (5), 'filled her whole being with a vague anguish' (8), 'summer meditations' (10), 'mazes of inward contemplation' (15), 'idly, aimlessly, unthinking and unguided' (18), 'drowsy, muffled sounds lulling her senses' (37), 'her whole existence was dulled, like a faded garment' (46), 'some unsought, extraneous impression' (56), 'a kind of reverie—a sort of stupor' (101). Edna's outer rebellion seems clearly charted, but her inner life is characterized as 'dream' and 'mood', presented as 'drift' not 'choice', a puzzled, vague passivity, mimicked perhaps in the frequency with which she falls asleep.

This passivity, inherent in the sentence structures, grammatical forms and vocabulary, reflects the difficulty of her inner transformation. The conflict between the outer and the inner life is made quite explicit: Edna 'began to *do* as she liked and to *feel* as she liked' (57: my emphasis). She considers 'her relations as an individual to the world within and about her', apprehending 'instinctively the dual life—that outward existence which conforms, the inward life which questions' (15). Initially she had welcomed outward conformity: as a wife 'she felt she would take her place with a certain dignity in the world of reality, closing the portals forever behind her upon the realms of romance and dreams' (19). But when Mr. Pontellier calls her to bed on the night she learns to swim, she begins

> to feel like one who awakens gradually out of a dream, a delicious, grotesque, impossible dream, to feel again the realities pressing into her soul . . . the conditions which crowded her in. (32)

Increasingly she chooses to open the portals and release the dreams and fantasies repressed since childhood, until eventually the inner life becomes more important than the outer:

> Edna looked straight before her with a self-absorbed expression upon her face. She felt no interest in anything about her. The street, the children, the fruit vender, the flowers growing there under her eyes, were all part and parcel of an alien world which had suddenly become antagonistic. (54)

It may seem that Edna is simply suffering, perhaps a little late in the century, the plight of the Romantic soul—'Every step . . . added to her strength and expansion as an individual'

(93)—a soul which eventually finds it impossible to subjugate its individuality to the common demands of life. Her resemblance to Emma Bovary; her espousal of a Bohemian life-style; her increasing pleasure in being alone[15]; the gradual breaking down of the reserve she had assumed as a girl; her growing reliance on her own judgement—all suggest a Romantic glorification of the self. In this reading of *The Awakening* Edna balances the respective demands of her newly acquired freedom with the demands of motherhood and cannot reconcile them; her fate is sealed by her presence at Mme. Ratignolle's confinement.[16] But this is to ignore the identity which Edna Pontellier discovers, and how that discovery condemns her to death.

The beginning of Edna's awakening is signalled by the first mention of her 'consciousness' which we are told is 'unfamiliar . . . vague . . . strange and unfamiliar' (28). Her growing awareness is surrounded by confused ambiguity:

> two contradictory impulses . . . impelled her.
> A certain light was beginning to dawn dimly within her,— the light which, showing the way, forbids it. . . .
> In short, Mrs. Pontellier was beginning to realize her position in the universe as a human being. . . .
> But the beginning of things . . . is necessarily vague, tangled, chaotic and exceedingly disturbing. (15)

At this stage Edna herself does not recognize what is happening:

> She could only realize that she herself—her present self—was in some way different from the other self. That she was seeing with different eyes and making the acquaintance of new conditions in herself that colored and changed her environment, she did not yet suspect. (41)

Soon she begins to take an active part in the process of discovery: 'She was seeking herself and finding herself in just such sweet, half-darkness which met her moods' (53). Others cannot understand the change: her husband 'could see plainly that she was not herself. That is, he could not see that she was becoming herself' (57). Increasingly now Edna questions what her true nature is. As her painting ' "grows in force and individuality" ' (79) she tells Arobin:

> I'm going to pull myself together for a while and think—try to determine what character of a woman I am; for, candidly, I don't

know. By all the codes which I am acquainted with, I am a devilishly wicked specimen of the sex. But some way I can't convince myself that I am. I must think about it. (82)

That night she sleeps with him and Chopin comments 'It was the first kiss of her life to which *her nature* had really responded' (83: my emphasis). Reflecting on her faithlessness to her husband, and more importantly, to Robert, she feels that '[a]bove all, there was understanding. She felt as if a mist had been lifted from her eyes, enabling her to look upon and comprehend the significance of life' (83). One of the indicators of Edna's passive ignorance ('mist') has been removed and she has accepted that sexuality is part of her nature. In the event it is not a very traumatic discovery.

> But among the conflicting sensations which assailed her, there was neither shame nor remorse. There was a dull pang of regret because it was not the kiss of love which had inflamed her, because it was not love which had held this cup of life to her lips. (83)

This is not the knowledge that will kill Edna. She has yet to learn something about herself that she cannot live with. When she reaches 'out for the unlimited in which to lose herself' (29), it is not because her 'suicide [originates] in a sense of inner emptiness'[17] but because of what she has discovered her true nature to be. To understand what that is we must turn to her past and her memory.[18]

The origins of Edna's crisis lie in her youth. Events from her past have moulded her response to the present: for example, the family is ' "of sound old Presbyterian Kentucky stock" ' (66) and her father ' "used to atone for his week-day sins with his Sunday devotions" ' (66)—an avenue which we have seen Edna herself explore briefly (see p. 50 above). Her father's visit foregrounds Edna's rôle as a daughter and the connection between her past and present. It is her father—whose ' "race horses literally ran away with the prettiest bit of Kentucky farming land" ' (66)—with whom she goes to the races where her liaison with Arobin develops. Edna

> was excited and in a manner radiant. She and her father had been to the race course. . . . [T]hey had met some very charming people. . . . Mrs. Mortimer Merriman and Mrs. James Highcamp,

who were with Alcée Arobin, had joined them and had enlivened the hours. (69)

On her second visit to the races Edna 'did not perceive that she was talking like her father as the sleek geldings ambled in review before them. She played for very high stakes' (74). Edna's affair will lose her her social birthright just as her father's gambling lost him his land.

Initially Edna rejects the belief that the past creates the present:

> For the first time she recognized anew the symptoms of infatuation which she had felt incipiently as a child, as a girl in her earliest teens, and later as a young woman. . . . The past was nothing to her; offered no lesson which she was willing to heed. The future was a mystery which she never attempted to penetrate. The present alone was significant; was hers. (46)

Before Edna herself becomes aware of it, the danger which the past holds for her is indicated symbolically in her reaction to the sight of Arobin's scar—a scar which shows that the past always leaves its mark, cannot be discarded.

> He felt the pressure of her pointed nails in the flesh of his palm. She arose hastily and walked toward the mantel. 'The sight of a wound or scar always agitates and sickens me,' she said. 'I shouldn't have looked at it.' (76)

The tragic ending to the story becomes inevitable when Edna looks at her own scars.

Surprised by the realization that she has been thinking of her youth in Kentucky and trying to understand what had stimulated the childhood memory, she connects it directly with the woman's current desire to learn to swim and thus with her awakening sexuality. Looking at the sea, Edna tries to recapture her thoughts:

> the sight of the water stretching so far away, those motionless sails against the blue sky, made a delicious picture that I just wanted to sit and look at. The hot wind beating in my face made me think—without any connection that I can trace—of a summer day in Kentucky, of a meadow that seemed as big as the ocean to the very little girl walking through the grass, which was higher than her waist. She threw out her arms as if swimming when she walked, beating the tall grass as one strikes out in the water. Oh, I see the connection now! (17)

The most important of Edna's memories are those of her
girlish passions for 'a dignified and sad-eyed cavalry officer who
visited her father, . . . a young gentleman who visited a lady on
a neighboring plantation' (18–19), 'a great tragedian . . . and a
few others' (19). She had hoped such emotional disturbances
had been banished by her marriage: 'She grew fond of her
husband, realizing with some unaccountable satisfaction that
no trace of passion . . . colored her affection, thereby threatening its dissolution' (19–20). But both her romantic attachment
to Robert and her affair with Arobin prove this a false hope.
What is worse she comes to believe that the pattern will
continue:

> 'Today it is Arobin; tomorrow it will be some one else'. . . . she
> realized that the day would come when [Robert], too, and the
> thought of him would melt out of her existence, leaving her alone.
> (113)

The Awakening rejects the Romantic faith in the individual
inasmuch as it rejects a belief in freedom of choice. The
identities which Edna thought she was free to choose or reject,
no longer seem possible as she comes to believe that her past
has formed and now defines her present self. For Edna, self-
realization and self-recognition converge:

> Edna felt as if she were being borne away from some anchorage
> which had held her fast, whose chains had been loosening—had
> snapped the night before when the mystic spirit was abroad,
> leaving her free to drift whithersoever she chose to set her sails.
> (35)

What had appeared to be choice was involuntary drift; Edna's
sails had been set long ago. Her final shocked awakening is not
to her present situation, but to the seamless continuity of her
old, present and future self.

When she enters the sea, Edna Pontellier is finally alone—
even the narrator has disappeared, leaving only a subjective
presentation of her consciousness. Edna is 'thinking of the
bluegrass meadow' and with the haunting final lines of the
book—'The spurs of the cavalry officer clanged as he walked
across the porch. There was the hum of bees, and the musky
odor of pinks filled the air' (114)—she tacitly acknowledges the
past as the cause of her suicide. She can no longer imagine a

future in which she would be other than the self she had hoped to abandon. It is paradoxical that the description of her death includes images of birth: she is 'like some new-born creature, opening its eyes in *a familiar world that it had never known*' (113: my emphasis). But the last eight words constitute a significant paradox: Edna would only wish to survive without the baggage of her own history and that can only be abandoned through death.

NOTES

1. Larzer Ziff, *The American 1890s: Life and Times of a Lost Generation* (New York: Viking Press, 1966), p. 304. Hereafter cited as Ziff. Kenneth Elbe, 'A Forgotten Novel: Kate Chopin's *The Awakening*', *Western Humanities Review*, 10 (Summer 1956), 263. Hereafter cited as Elbe.
2. Paula A. Treichler, 'The Construction of Ambiguity in *The Awakening*: A Linguistic Analysis', in *Woman and Language in Literature and Society*, ed. Sally McConnell-Ginet *et al.* (New York: Praeger Publishers, 1980), p. 249. Hereafter cited as Treichler. Barbara C. Ewell, *Kate Chopin* (New York: Ungar Publishing Company, 1986), p. 145. My emphasis.
3. Kate Chopin, *The Awakening*, ed. Margaret Culley (New York: Norton & Company, 1976), p. 35. All subsequent quotations will be from this edition.
4. Joan Zlotnick, 'A Woman's Will: Kate Chopin on Selfhood, Wifehood, and Motherhood', *Markham Review*, 3 (October 1968), 4. Hereafter cited as Zlotnick.
5. Ziff, p. 300.
6. Emily Toth, 'The Independent Woman and "Free" Love', *Massachusetts Review*, 16 (Autumn 1981), 658.
7. Edna's progression to nakedness is clearly charted. She is seen initially under a parasol and then with progressively fewer clothes on. Equally significantly her name also changes from Mrs. Pontellier to Edna Pontellier to Edna as she rejects socially imposed identities.
8. The concept of women as property spreads in other directions too. Immediately after the passage quoted, Edna acknowledges her subordinate position by mutely asking for, receiving and putting on her rings—rings which presumably include the wedding ring which defines her and which she later tries to crush. Mr. Pontellier's affection for Edna is part of his pride in ownership: he 'greatly valued his possessions, chiefly because they were his, and derived genuine pleasure from contemplating a painting, a statuette . . .—no matter what—after he had bought it and placed it among his household gods' (50). It is in this context that we must understand Edna's response to Robert's reference to ' "men who had set

their wives free".... "I am no longer one of Mr. Pontellier's possessions to dispose of or not. I give myself where I choose"' (106–97).

9. The most pervasive example of this relationship lies in the dual nature of the sea and Edna's learning to swim in it. When the sexual metaphor of swimming becomes an actual experience, and when Edna actually drowns herself in an image of the unattainable, the reader is understandably disoriented.

10. George Spangler, 'Kate Chopin's *The Awakening*: A Partial Dissent', *Novel: A Forum on Fiction*, 3 (Spring 1970), 251. Zlotnick, p. 3. Elbe, p. 267. Donald A. Ringe, 'Romantic Imagery in Kate Chopin's *The Awakening*', *American Literature*, 43 (January 1972), 588.

11. The portrait of Edna is frequently internalized. When 'Edna was a little miss, just merging into her teens ... the realization that she herself was nothing, nothing, nothing to the engaged young man was a bitter affliction' (19); the intensity in the repetition of 'nothing' signifies our entry into her consciousness. The use of reported speech after Robert has announced his imminent departure ('Victor ... thanked his mother.... Monsieur Farival thought.... Victor thought.... Madame Lebrun grew a trifle hysterical; Robert called his brother some sharp, hard names' (42)) indicates our identification with Edna's numbed incomprehension.

12. Treichler, pp. 239–40.

13. Treichler, p. 241.

14. Cynthia Griffin Wolff, 'Thanatos and Eros: Kate Chopin's *The Awakening*', *American Quarterly*, 25 (October 1973), 466. Hereafter cited as Wolff. Mr. Pontellier is characterized by 'strong' words— 'property ... right ... straight' (3), 'instructed' (5), 'information' (7), 'disapproval ... remonstrance' (92). He, of course, is secure in his position; Edna has yet to discover hers.

15. Her need to be alone inexorably intensifies. She tells her husband ' "Let me alone; you bother me"' (57), 'she liked then to wander alone ... she found it good to dream and to be alone and unmolested' (58), 'a radiant peace settled upon her when she at last found herself alone. Even the children were gone' (72). 'There was something in her attitude, in her whole appearance ... which suggested the regal woman, the one who rules, who looks on, who stands alone' (88). She tells Doctor Mandelet ' "I'm not going to be forced into doing things.... I want to be let alone"' (109)—until finally 'she had come alone.... The voice of the sea is seductive ... inviting the soul to wander in abysses of solitude.... she was there beside the sea, absolutely alone' (112–13). In manuscript the novel was entitled 'A Solitary Soul'.

16. It would not be correct to suggest that Edna's uneasiness in her rôle as mother is unimportant to her concept of herself and thus in her suicide. Early in the book we are told that 'She was fond of her children in an uneven, impulsive way. She would sometimes gather them passionately to her heart; she would sometimes forget them.... Their absence was a sort of relief, though she did not admit this, even to herself. It seemed to free her of a responsibility which she had blindly assumed and for which Fate had not fitted her' (20). This feeling is reinvoked after the birth of

Madame Ratignolle's baby when Doctor Mandelet, echoing Edna's incoherent thoughts, says ' "The trouble is . . . that youth is given up to illusions. It seems to be a provision of Nature; a decoy to secure mothers for the race" ' (109–10). Her statement to Madame Ratignolle—'that she would never sacrifice herself for her children. . . . "I would give my life for my children; but I wouldn't give myself" ' (48)—is also echoed at the end of the book. 'The children appeared before her like antagonists who had overcome her; who had overpowered and sought to drag her into the soul's slavery for the rest of her days. But she knew a way to elude them. . . . They were a part of her life. But they need not have thought that they could possess her, body and soul' (113–14). In both cases the important change is not in Edna's attitude to being a mother—indeed it is important to recognize that it is quite clearly the same—but in her new ability to do something about the problem.

17. Wolff, p. 469.
18. 'Desirée's Baby' and 'A Lady of Bayou St. John' provide other examples of Chopin using the past as the formative element of identity.

4

Making Room for the Artist in Edith Wharton's *Old New York*

by SHARON SHALOO

Edith Wharton's *Old New York* comprises four novellas: *False Dawn: The 'Forties*; *The Old Maid: The 'Fifties*; *The Spark: The 'Sixties*; and *New Year's Day: The 'Seventies*.[1] The tales unfold a decade-by-decade chronicle of society life in mid- to late-nineteenth-century New York City. Among Wharton's last published attempts at the genre, the novellas were written over a period of four years, from 1920 to 1924. Three appeared individually in periodicals as they were completed; and the four were published under the collective title *Old New York* in 1924, as a boxed set of individually clothbound volumes.[2] This innovative first edition, thus, acknowledges the integrity of each volume while it affirms the strength of the vision that binds them together.

Unfortunately, Wharton's readers have not always viewed *Old New York* quite in this light. Discussions have often focused on one or another of the volumes (that one being, most often, *False Dawn* or *The Old Maid*, at the expense of *The Spark* and *New Year's Day*), or have blurred the distinctions among the volumes by reading them as four instalments of the same dramatic situation.[3] The present account seeks to re-emphasize the format of the first edition by looking at the discrete fictions that comprise *Old New York* and by considering the collected whole they represent. In addition, it intends to explore the ways in which this work marks not so much the end of Wharton's great beginning as, instead, the beginning of her great end.

A due regard for Wharton's achievement in these novellas has not been helped by the widespread opinion that Wharton's literary powers went into decline after the publication in 1920 of *The Age of Innocence*.[4] Given this critical assumption, well-intentioned attempts to find value in *Old New York* usually proceed by comparing it with those early works thought to be Wharton's best: *The House of Mirth* (1905), *Ethan Frome* (1911), *The Reef* (1912), *The Custom of the Country* (1913), and *The Age of Innocence* (1920).[5] *False Dawn* and *The Old Maid* are most 'like' those early works, which present, in her early and influential advocate Blake Nevius's terms, fictional dramas of the trapped consciousness; and in these two novellas is often detected the last gasp of Wharton's artistic voice.

Granted, *Old New York* begins by reworking the themes of Wharton's earlier period, her dramas of trapped consciousness. Yet it ends, demonstrably, with a show of the themes she was to explore during the last fifteen years of her life. As the collection develops, we find it moving away from the suffocating atmospheres of *False Dawn* and *The Old Maid*. It wends its way toward more productive spaces in *The Spark* and *New Year's Day*, considering, along the way, the nature of literary creativity and the possibility of sexual fulfilment, and considering those issues, moreover, in terms that clearly reflect factors and impulses drawn from Wharton's own life. Indeed, as *Old New York* closes, we begin to hear murmurings of the thesis Wharton would soon come to argue, that inspiration lay in the territory where literary creativity and sexual fulfilment converge.

Wharton initially planned to publish two novellas under the title 'Among the Mingotts', thus intending links between characters in the novellas and Mrs. Manson Mingott, one of the most appealing characters in *The Age of Innocence*. In all likelihood, Wharton conceived of these fictions while writing *The Age of Innocence*. She completed *The Old Maid* in 1921. *New Year's Day* followed in 1922, and should have completed 'Among the Mingotts'. Had she stopped there, Wharton would have produced two novellas that comment upon each other and, together, upon *The Age of Innocence*: *The Old Maid* traces a May Welland-like Delia Ralston through the strains of a conventional life, and *New Year's Day* discloses the much maligned but essentially irreproachable isolation of an Ellen-Olenska figure in Lizzie Hazeldean. Apart from their collection, then, these novellas dramatize the sensibilities of the sorts of female characters obscured by and subordinated to Newland Archer's limited centre of vision in *The Age of Innocence*.

Somewhere along the line, however, 'Among the Mingotts' became *Old New York*. *False Dawn* and *The Spark* followed in 1923 and 1924, and the collection developed beyond the concerns of Wharton's earlier novel. With them, Wharton seems to have initiated an investigation of the literary artist, a figure she would explore in the essays comprising *The Writing of Fiction* (1925), in the novels *Hudson River Bracketed* (1929) and *The Gods Arrive* (1932), and in her autobiographical *A Backward Glance* (1934). For these novellas are punctuated by the figures of American men of letters: Edgar Allan Poe's name is whispered in the early morning of *False Dawn*, and Walt Whitman is an inspirational force in *The Spark*.

At first glance, Poe's and Whitman's places in the collection seem intentionally marginal, as if they are there simply to criticize the artistic tastes of late-nineteenth-century New York society. Wharton notes in her autobiography that such 'ungentlemanly' artists were banished from genteel libraries for reasons closely resembling those for which Poe and Whitman are criticized in the pages of *Old New York*: they were called 'jingoists' or 'atheists'; their work was considered 'rubbish' or 'immoral'.[6] Yet Poe and Whitman are literary lions whose work influenced Wharton's own. In fact, she once claimed, 'Those two, with Emerson, are the best that we have—in fact, the all we have' (Lewis, 236). In *Old New York*, Wharton creates one or two characters who might be included among the 'we' in her appreciative claim who 'have' these artists: in *False Dawn* Lewis Raycie has heard Poe read his poetry; in *The Spark* the narrator has put Whitman in his library. Poe and Whitman are included, therefore, in the artistic discourse of these novellas. Indeed, Poe's influence echoes throughout the collection and Whitman's inspiration can be seen at its core. With Poe's and Whitman's aid, we can trace the ways in which the novellas of *Old New York* search for secure and nurturing space, space which, once found, will provide safe haven for the artistic sensibilities that are threatened by a privileged but undeniably genteel and mercantile social *milieu*. These literary figures provide terms for assessing the spaces inhabited by characters in the novellas and for judging the extent to which Wharton's 'we'—fellow citizens of her republic of the spirit, a literary and cultural republic to which she proudly pledges allegiance in *A Backward Glance*— can be said to have found sanctuary in *Old New York*.

The suggestion to view *Old New York* as an announcement of themes to come is not untoward, for Wharton often investigates new ideas in her novellas. To take early examples, *The Touchstone* (1900; published in England as *A Gift from the Grave*) watches a young man publish for profit the love letters of a famous novelist, a woman who bore to the grave her unrequited love for the unworthy protagonist. This novella is shortly followed by another, *Sanctuary* (1903), which tells the story of a woman who marries an ignoble man, not to reform him but, instead, to establish herself as a guiding moral force for any children he may sire. These tales investigate two versions of self-sacrifice, outlining situations their author would take up again, more complexly and to much greater effect, in *The House of Mirth*. There, the heroine, Lily Bart, avoids the temptation to publish what should remain private when she burns love letters that have come into her possession. Additionally, and to her ruin, Lily cannot bring herself to sacrifice her 'self' in marriage to a man unworthy of respect. Then, in the novella *Madame de Treymes* (1907), Wharton explores the negative aspects of a French aristocracy that emphasizes family and tradition at the expense of personal freedom and happiness. She depicts these aristocratic habits in generally better hues in the figure of Raymond de Chelles in *The Custom of the Country*, the novel she was composing at the time *Madame de Treymes* was published. As we have seen, *The Old Maid* and *New Year's Day* originated in a dialogue with another of Wharton's novels, *The Age of Innocence*.

Perhaps it is their dependency on the novels or the preliminary nature of their investigations that leads Wharton to devalue her shorter fictions. Clearly, her bias is with her novels. In *A Backward Glance* (1934), which she was planning if not actually writing as she composed *Old New York*, Wharton makes her prejudice clear. Rehearsing her feelings upon publication of her first book, a collection of stories titled *The Greater Inclination* (1899), she says,

> At last I had groped my way through to my vocation, and thereafter never questioned that story-telling was my job, though I doubted whether I should be able to cross the chasm which separated the *nouvelle* from the novel.[7]

In *The Writing of Fiction* (1925), a collection of essays written contemporaneously with and published shortly after *Old New York*, Wharton distinguishes between the two forms in phrases that explain why she was determined to cross that chasm: 'The short story is an improvisation, the temporary shelter of a flitting fancy, compared to the four-square and deeply founded monument which the novel ought to be.'[8] She admits some merit to the concise, dramatic foreshortening of events that she feels is the *raison d'être* of the short story, but she values more highly the complex variations that can be achieved in the effort of a novel.

If *The Writing of Fiction* undervalues the short story, it dismisses the novella altogether. While it devotes a chapter to 'Telling a Short Story', two chapters to 'Constructing a Novel' and 'Character and Situation in the Novel', and another two to thoughts 'In General' and to the achievement of 'Marcel Proust', *The Writing of Fiction*, by this author of at least nine and perhaps as many as thirteen novellas,[9] yields but one sentence to their form:

> Meanwhile, it may be pointed out that a third, and intermediate, form of tale—the *long* short story—is available for any subject too spreading for conciseness yet too slight in texture to be stretched into a novel.[10]

In Edith Wharton's literary theory the novella occupies negative ground, its territory defined chiefly by the failure of a subject to meet the demands of concision on the one hand or complexity on the other.

'Failure' is a key word here. Consider, for example, Wharton's early assessment of *Ethan Frome*. During the composition of what was to become her most widely read fiction, Wharton reported cheerfully to her friend Bernard Berenson that 'the *nouvelle* . . . has grown into a large long-legged hobbledehoy of a young novel. 20,000 long it is already, and growing.' To Berenson's later inquiry after the young novel, however, she lamented, 'My "novel" doesn't deserve the name. It is a hybrid, or rather dwarf form, of the species: scarcely 40,000 words' (Lewis, p. 297). Her disappointment is palpable. Later, she manages to recuperate *Ethan Frome*, but only as an exercise well-executed. She says, 'It was not until I wrote "Ethan Frome" that I suddenly felt the artisan's full control of his implements'; yet she maintains that she is 'far from thinking "Ethan Frome" [her] best [work]' (*Glance*, p. 209). Wharton wants her work to measure up and invites us to view her novels as the cornerstones of her art. Nevertheless, it is in her novellas that we find Wharton laying her foundations.

As *Old New York* opens, for example, *False Dawn: The 'Forties* follows the progress of a son of old New York, Lewis Raycie, who is about to embark on his Grand Tour. His father surprises him on the eve of his departure with a welcome charge: the elder Raycie has established an account from which Lewis is to draw funds for the purchase of paintings that will form the basis of a Raycie Gallery. Mr. Raycie instructs his son to contact various dealers throughout Europe but essentially gives him carte blanche on purchases. Herein lies the problem. While Lewis Raycie sets out with many of his father's artistic assumptions, he soon will come under the influence of others— of one John Ruskin, whom he meets in the Alps, and of certain other Englishmen, including William Morris and Dante Gabriel Rossetti. The reader is given early hints of this impending clash in Raycie tastes.

Lewis Raycie thinks Poe 'a Great Poet', though he merely whispers that opinion to his sister, in the early morning hours, outside the pantry of the Raycie summer house. By contrast, in the elder Raycie's study, 'a small bare and formidable room' (Pt. I, Ch. 2, p. 51), Poe is ranked among 'certain blasphemous penny-a-liners whose poetic ravings are said to have given them a kind of pothouse notoriety'. In that room, Lewis Raycie merely 'redden[s] at the allusion but [is] silent'. His incipient artistic sensibility is not forceful enough to insert a controversial cultural opinion into the conversations that dominate the world of his father's study. Raycie's early belief in Poe's achievement, like his later belief in the Italian paintings he will collect with

Ruskin's aid, will have to be vindicated by another.

On his return from Europe, laden with Piero della Francescas, Gioto da Bondones, and Carpaccios rather than the Carlo Dolces, Giulio Romanos, and Sassoferratos his father values, Raycie tries to sway his father with rather Emersonian arguments, 'pleading the cause he had hoped his pictures would have pleaded for him, dethroning the old Powers and Principalities, and setting up these new names in their place' (Pt. II, Ch. 6, p. 93). He meets with no success, however. His paintings will not as yet fetch a high price in his father's world, and dollars are the only measure of value available to the elder Mr. Raycie. For the remainder of *False Dawn*, the younger Raycie awaits the arrival of 'the one who knows', the one, in other words, who will proclaim the merit in his unfashionable artistic tastes. Unfortunately, that one does not arrive in Lewis Raycie's lifetime. The paintings he brought to light from Italian grottoes are condemned to hang in galleries no one visits and then to be stored in attics no one explores. The paintings, like Lewis Raycie himself, suffer the consequences of old New York's prejudices. In the final irony, of course, when the one who knows—'a quiet fellow connected with the Louvre'—does arrive, in a subsequent generation, to announce the value of the Italian primitives, New York society quickly converts that value to capital by auctioning off the art. The primitives are thus expelled from the world Raycie would have had them educate. In all ways, then, young Raycie's sensibilities marked a false dawn for culture in old New York.

Edgar Allan Poe defines the artistic atmosphere of *False Dawn*. Obviously, his works represent the grottoes and attics that hide Raycie's Italian paintings for most of the novella. Moreover, as the tale opens we find this literary artist exiled to obscure poverty somewhere in the Bronx, packed away, like Raycie's primitives, where 1840s New York might ignore him. Significantly, Poe's influence does not end with the close of the tale. Like the rescued paintings, it escapes 1840s New York. In particular, those who know Poe's 'Philosophy of Furniture' will find in the essay a critical language with which to evaluate the public and private spaces negotiated by the central characters of *The Old Maid* and *New Year's Day*.

The Old Maid: The 'Fifties follows two cousins, Delia Ralston (née Lovell) and Charlotte Lovell, from young adulthood to old age. Each of the women was once attached to the struggling artist Clement Spender, who left New York for Rome, the site of artistic possibility in this novella as it was in *False Dawn*. Delia denied her feelings for Spender, made a conventional marriage to a prominent New Yorker, James Ralston, and settled into material comfort and domestic tranquility in fashionable Gramercy Park. While Delia repressed her passion, Charlotte Lovell indulged hers. She was the woman to whom Spender turned for solace after Delia's marriage. As a result, Charlotte bore an illegitimate daughter, Tina, whose existence is made known to Delia only as the novella opens. Delia's lingering regret for Spender is quickly transformed into a maternal longing for Tina; and during the course of the novella, she will vie with Charlotte for ascendancy in relation to the child. Each cousin seeks through Tina to atone for her earlier disappointments: Delia would have Tina experience her passionate nature; Charlotte would have her repress it. In an unsatisfactory compromise, as the novella closes we find that the cousins have succeeded in providing this child of an artist with a radically questioned domestic ideal.

The Old Maid opens in Delia Ralston's bedroom:

> [Delia] glanced complacently at the French wallpaper that reproduced a watered silk, with a "valanced" border, and tassels between the loops. The mahogany bedstead, covered with a white embroidered counterpane, was symmetrically reflected in the mirror of a wardrobe which matched it. Coloured lithographs . . . surmounted groups of family daguerreotypes in deeply-recessed gilt frames. (Pt. I, Ch. 1, p. 16)

This carefully composed room is, according to the principles Edgar Allan Poe argues in 'Philosophy of Furniture', decidedly wanting in 'keeping'. In such a room, Poe says, 'straight lines are too prevalent—too uninterruptedly continued—or clumsily interrupted at right angles. If curved lines occur, they are repeated into unpleasant uniformity.' For Poe, the colourless surface of Delia's bedroom mirror would be doubly regrettable since it reflects the blanched counterpane on the bedstead. Moreover, the room lacks intimacy. The description is devoid of personal or possessive pronouns and stops short of detailing the carpet, which Poe terms the 'soul' of a room. The decoration of this room, as of other 'well-appointed apartments' in America's aristocracy of wealth, confounds, as Poe would say, the ideas of magnificence and beauty.[11] Delia characterizes her room as 'pretty' when, in fact, she means 'costly'. This ostensibly private room is intended to communicate a public message of material security, a security Delia gained in her marriage to James Ralston. Significantly, the Ralston family power is displayed in daguerreotypes on the wall, deeply embedded in heavily gilted frames.

While it is secure, Delia's is not nurturing space. Her bedroom is, in every respect, a passionless room. As she recalls her wedding night, Delia remembers the 'startled puzzled surrender to the incomprehensible exigencies of the young man'; she reviews,

> the evasions, insinuations, resigned smiles and Bible texts of one's Mama; the reminder of the phrase 'to obey' in the glittering blur of the Marriage Service; a week or a month of flushed distress, confusion, embarrassed pleasure; then the growth of habit, the insidious lulling of the matter of course, the dreamless double slumbers in the big white bed, the early morning consultations through that dressing-room door which had once seemed to open into a fiery pit scorching the brow of innocence. (Pt. I, Ch. 1, pp. 14–15)

Glaringly absent from her recollections are images of bodies, of touch, of sexuality. Delia reconstitutes the scene of her 'surrender' in images of sleep and of domestic discussion, thus banishing the chaos of desire by extinguishing the red fires of passion that threatened to burn the white brow of innocence.

Charlotte Lovell has inhabited very different rooms, ones the matronly yet, paradoxically, sexually naïve Delia cannot envision until she sees Tina arriving home late one night, escorted only by her suitor:

> [N]ow, at a glance, [Delia] understood. How often Charlotte Lovell, staying alone in town with her infirm grandmother, must have walked home from evening parties with Clement Spender, how often have let herself and him into the darkened house, . . . where there was no one to spy upon their coming and going. . . . Delia . . . saw the grim drawing-room which had been their moonlit forest, . . . with its swathed chandelier and hard Empire

sofas, and the eyeless marble caryatids of the mantel; she pictured the shaft of moonlight falling across the swans and garlands of the faded carpet, and in that icy light two young figures in each others' arms. (Pt. II, Ch. 9, pp. 136–38)

Not Poe's ideal room in which 'repose' is all, this room manages, nevertheless, a closer approximation than did Delia's bedroom: reprehensible chandeliers and sofas are draped with covers, unfortunate patterns in the carpet are faded. Poe's ethereal beauty of 'three or four female heads' is gestured to in the marble caryatids and, most significantly, no excess of drapery prevents the rays of the moon from illuminating the embrace of two figures. Yet, Charlotte's room is but a stolen corner, draped only for fleeting evenings. Her liaison may have momentarily turned the world of *The Old Maid* upside down, but it did not precipitate social revolution.

Delia's movement from the image of the marital bed to that of the hard Empire sofa, from the safe and secure rooms above to the tumult of those below, is a movement toward knowledge but not toward liberation. For Charlotte, like Delia, is loyal to the conventional restraints under which she suffers. The technique of the double heroine here—as in many of Wharton's novels—is not employed to validate one character over another. Rather, Wharton splits advantages between Delia and Charlotte; any hope for an ideal is banished to the chasm separating them; and both are doomed to a world of constricted possibilities. Significantly, toward the close of their tale, we see the two climbing the stairs together, Charlotte checking her 'impetuous step' to keep time with the speed Delia can manage with her 'stiffened joints'.

Delia Ralston and Charlotte Lovell have devoted their lives to the production of the ideal (passionate and secure) marriage each of them was denied. And at first glance Tina's marriage seems to reward their efforts. But the novella finally laments their actions. For the cousins conspire to undermine the forces of family that would deny an illegitimate child a marriage; yet they do so by secreting Charlotte's maternity and having Delia legally adopt Tina. Thus they deny the legitimacy of a passionate liaison with an artistic sensibility; they rebel only to the extent necessary to provide Tina with the opportunity to conform.

Tina's marriage only momentarily transforms the drawing-room of Lovell Place, Delia's summer house, into a rose-filled, lace-hung chapel. As Delia well knows, 'On the following evening the house will be empty: till death came, she and Charlotte would sit alone together beside the evening lamp' (Pt. II, Ch. 11, p. 170). She and Charlotte will remain trapped in a world that is very nearly obsolete, in drawing-rooms that

> kept their slender settees, their Sheraton consoles and cabinets [because it] had been thought useless to discard them for more fashionable furniture, since the growth of the city made it certain that the place must eventually be sold. (Pt. II, Ch. 11, p. 168)

The scene of Tina's wedding is a house destined for extinction; it is not generative space.

While *The Old Maid* moves from Delia Ralston's curiously public bedroom through images of nearly abandoned drawing-rooms, *New Year's Day: The 'Seventies* moves in an opposite and much more hopeful direction, taking its protagonist through troublesome drawing-rooms to a private haven in a bedroom. In this novella, the drawing-room is the scene of the social ostracism of its protagonist, Lizzie Hazeldean. The first drawing-room one encounters is Mrs. Parrett's, from which vantage point Lizzie is observed emerging one New Year's Day from the burning Fifth Avenue Hotel. She is in the company of Henry Prest, with whom she has long been suspected of having an affair. The fiction moves to Mrs. Struthers's drawing-room that evening for Lizzie's public damnation. Even the drawing-room in which her husband, Charles Hazeldean, proposed to her is compromised. Six months after her husband's death, Henry Prest visits Lizzie in the room, offering, as he says, 'to regularize' their 'attachment' in marriage (Ch. 6, p. 108). Had she agreed to the match, of course, old New York would have forgotten her indiscretions as they earlier forgot Tina Lovell Ralston's hazy lineage. *New Year's Day* would have been, in other words, as hopeless as Tina's wedding night. Instead, Lizzie seals her own isolation by refusing Prest's offer and by confessing to him, moreover, that she had never loved him but had essentially prostituted herself to him for his money. She announces herself ready to suffer the consequences of her social rebellion.

Ironically, for a woman of tarnished reputation, Lizzie's bedroom is the least compromised space in the novella. She retreats to it after her fateful New Year's assignation with Prest:

> It was a rosy room, hung with one of the new English chintzes, which also covered the deep sofa, and the bed with its rose-lined pillow-covers. The carpet was cherry red, the toilet-table ruffled and looped like a ball dress. Ah, how she and Susan had ripped and sewn and hammered, and pieced together old scraps of lace and ribbon and muslin, in the making of that airy monument! (Ch. 2, pp. 31–2)

She has decorated her room with the consummate good taste and predominant crimsons Poe detailed in his ideal room. In this room, however, 'repose' is not yet all. The vivid flowers that Poe says blend so well with the decoration of this room jar effectively on Lizzie's nerves. Henry Prest sent them. Henry Prest, in fact, is responsible for the entire room. It is his money and not, as she tells Charles, her stepmother's that Lizzie uses to remodel her bedroom. Yet, she creates this 'airy monument' for her husband's benefit, for his pleasure and peace of mind concerning her future financial well-being. The novella takes as its primary task the resolution in Lizzie Hazeldean's favour of the contradictions of this space.

The first words of *New Year's Day* are spoken by the narrator's mother, who condemns Lizzie Hazeldean: 'She was *bad* . . . always. They used to meet at the Fifth Avenue Hotel' (Ch. 1, p. 3). The mother's stern disapproval opens the fiction figuratively as well, for it prompts the narrator to pursue Lizzie's story. He investigates the meaning of 'She was *bad* . . . always', testing its veracity and measuring its consequences for the character who becomes, in the process, his protagonist. His resultant summation of Lizzie's past departs sharply from his mother's. He says, 'She had done one great—or abominable—thing; rank it as you please' (Ch. 7, p. 150). His alternative, then, to his mother's dismissal is not another monologic morality but, instead, a fictionalizing process that investigates absolutes and finds them wanting. What is more, by incorporating the narrative of Christian salvation into the language of his tale, the narrator challenges the authority with which his mother levels her judgement.

On his return from a year of travel, the narrator finds Lizzie Hazeldean, his old friend by this point in the tale, taking comfort from a priest:

> [The priest], who understood her so well, could . . . tell her things about Charles: knew where he was, how he felt, what exquisite daily attentions could still be paid to him, and how, with all unworthiness washed away, she might at last hope to reach him. . . . The house no longer seemed lonely, nor the hours tedious; there had even been found for her, among the books she had so often tried to read, those books which had so long looked at her with such hostile faces, two or three (they were always on her bed) containing messages from the world where Charles was waiting.
>
> Thus provided and led, one day she went to him. (Ch. 7, pp. 159–60)

The priest's narrative, in collusion with the narrator's intentions, creates a sanctified space. Most particularly, the bedroom has become Lizzie's safe haven from her long-suffered isolation. In moving her from the condemnation of the drawing-room to the absolution of the bedroom, the novella has moved from public to private space and from constraint toward liberation. In doing so, the tale has moved away from the world of drawing-room morality toward another world in which judgements are not levelled so readily or so unequivocably. It is no mistake that Lizzie Hazeldean is provided with several books in her peaceful bedroom, for the movement from public constraint to private liberation is, for Wharton, a movement toward art.

In *A Backward Glance*, Wharton describes a time when, as a young woman, she finally gathered the courage to ask her mother about the history of a particular cousin, George Alfred, whose name was always spoken in disapproving terms:

> 'But, Mama, what did he do?' 'Some woman'—my mother muttered: and no one accustomed to the innocuous word as now used can imagine the shades of disapproval, scorn and yet excited curiosity, that 'some' could then connote on the lips of virtue.
>
> George Alfred—and some woman! . . . Who was she? . . . To her respectable sisters her culpability was as certain in advance as Predestination to a Calvinist. . . . The vision of poor featureless unknown Alfred and his siren, lurking in some cranny of my

imagination, hinted at regions perilous, dark, and yet lit with mysterious fires, just outside the world of copy-book axioms, and the old obediences that were in my blood; and the hint was useful—for a novelist. (*Glance*, pp. 24–5)

Wharton reconstructs her response to her mother's dismissal of 'some woman' as an imaginative flight toward the taboo, toward an inspirational territory her mother would prefer to leave unexplored and insufficiently described in her loaded phrase, just as the mother of *New Year's Day* would have preferred to end Lizzie Hazeldean's story at its beginning, with 'She was bad . . . always.'

Walt Whitman is the literary figure who provides Wharton with a model for her pursuit of the ostracized protagonist. Lizzie Hazeldean, if not Wharton's Mary Magdalene, is the central figure in Wharton's prose homage to Whitman's 'To a Common Prostitute', whose poet addresses his subject as follows:

> Not till the sun excludes you do I exclude you,
> Not till the waters refuse to glisten for you and the leaves
> to rustle for you, do my words refuse to glisten
> and rustle for you.[12]

Wharton's narrator, like Whitman's poet, will tell the stories of women whom the mothers of old New York would have her ignore. Indeed, Whitman's influence seems to have been woven into the fabric of *Old New York*. Most suggestively, the poet is introduced in the novella titled *The Spark: The 'Sixties*. This novella marks the decade of inspiration, of Wharton's actual birth into old New York and of her figurative birth into her republic of the spirit, and Walt Whitman is its guiding force.

The central figure of *The Spark*, Hayley Delane, carries with him the image of Whitman's selfless volunteer effort during the American Civil War; this youthful memory prompts the adult Delane to similar acts of kindness, even when those attempts to alleviate suffering are criticized by his small, privileged social set. The novella is careful, however, to identify the limits of Whitman's influence on Delane. The closing action of *The Spark* takes place in its narrator's library. Hayley Delane drops by to visit and, having tired of the newspapers, uncharacteristically picks up a book he finds lying open on a reading table. To his delight, he discovers a portrait of the old gray-bearded man whose memory he cherishes—on the frontispiece of a late edition of *Leaves of Grass*. Initially astonished, Delane is finally disconcerted to learn that his 'old pal from Washington' wrote the volume. In fact, in the closing words of the novella, Delane reproaches the narrator for revealing that 'Old Walt' wrote 'all that rubbish'. Delane's literary sensibilities are determined by the late-eighteenth- and early-nineteenth-century verse he learned in his youth. He cannot displace the old Powers and Principalities of poetry to grasp the beauty of Whitman's new verse forms. Whitman has spoken to Delane's social commitment, with a message that 'we're working out toward something better' (Ch. 4, p. 71); but the poet has not reached him aesthetically.

Finally, however, Delane's literary sensibilities are not central to *The Spark*. It is the narrator of this novella, after all, whose library includes *Leaves of Grass*. It is the narrator, too, perhaps inspired by the democratic vistas Whitman scanned, who pays homage to Hayley Delane's humanitarian acts. His portrait of Delane is, he says,

> an attempt to depict for you—and in so doing, perhaps make clearer for myself—the aspect and character of a man whom I loved, perplexedly but faithfully, for many years. (Ch. 3, pp. 41–2)

The narrator's relationship to Delane is, thus, emotional and critical at the same time. The narrator lives in Delane's world but is not of it; he maintains the distance necessary to evaluate the character he admires. Delane is to him what Lizzie is to the narrator who follows: a literary subject.

The narrator of *The Spark* is one of the most valued representatives of Wharton's republic of the spirit to be encountered among the characters of *Old New York*. For in choosing a profession in New York banking, he has not relinquished intellectual freedom or artistic inclination. Like the narrator who follows in *New Year's Day*, he does not become trapped by the forces that ruin Lewis Raycie, Delia Ralston, or Charlotte Lovell. Neither is he limited in artistic scope as was the elder Mr. Raycie or Hayley Delane. Like Lizzie Hazeldean, he occupies privileged space beyond the threats of constraint that convention attempts to level at the unconventional. As with Lizzie Hazeldean, his movement beyond constraint is a movement toward art.

Not coincidentally, this narrator's safe haven is the library of a reader. From within that room he inserts Whitman's poetry into the narrative of old New York. In this way, *The Spark* pays tribute to Whitman's art; it creates an imaginative space in which his poetry can flourish and gives the poet his due by giving him his audience. Furthermore, this narrator and the one who follows him in *New Year's Day* are, like Whitman's poet, artists of the New World. Rather than relying on a Grand Tour of Europe or fleeing to a studio in Rome, these narrators create a possibility for art in old New York. *The Spark* and *New Year's Day*, thus, suggest that those 'ones who know', those citizens of Wharton's republic of the spirit, may have begun to take up residency in the houses of old New York.

Edith Wharton counts herself among those readers and writers who are moved by Walt Whitman, and she links her social and literary development with his. Socially, she finds analogies between her volunteer efforts during the Great War— for which France awarded her a medal of the Legion of Honour— and the charitable work Whitman earlier performed. More pertinently, Wharton describes her first literary inspiration as a time when 'the grasses first spoke to [her]' (*Glance*, p. 4) and takes the title for her own autobiography, *A Backward Glance*, from Whitman's autobiographical 'A Backward Glance O'er Travel'd Roads'. This allusion signals what may be Whitman's greatest influence on Wharton. In its imaginative recreation of autobiographical experience, Whitman's *Leaves of Grass* provides a model that Wharton follows not only in the collection at hand but also in many of the works that follow it. Indeed, *Old New York*, in its evolution from individual pieces to a collective work, and in the development of literary sensibility the fictions trace, might well be seen as Edith Wharton's own *Leaves of Grass*, in which she obliquely sings a song of herself.

At the margins of the individual tales one encounters allusions to characters and events from the author's life. Lewis Raycie secretly courts Treeshy Kent in the manner that Edith Wharton's father devised for visiting her mother. Wharton's mother's début in turned garments and hand-me-down slippers is repeated in the societal appearance of Charlotte Lovell, a long-suffering and unacknowledged mother. Hayley Delane voices a reverence for the proper use of the English language that Edith Wharton would repeat in describing her early training in the language her parents revered. The New Year's Day Fifth Avenue Hotel fire, which forces a stream of women of questionable taste onto the street, may be Wharton's last laugh on Mrs. Paran Stevens, widow of the owner of the Fifth Avenue Hotel. Mrs. Stevens was the mother of Harry Stevens, to whom Edith Wharton was once engaged and with whom she had to break, reportedly at Mrs. Stevens' instigation. Most personally, Wharton grants Lizzie Hazeldean a line that she once used in her private diary, in reference to the end of her affair with Morton Fullerton: 'I've had my day . . . no woman has more than one' (Lewis, pp. 207–32).

Most resonantly, the overall movement of the collection is analogous to the movement Wharton charts for herself in her autobiography. The artist moves from Italy to New York, just as Wharton moves from *The Valley of Decision*, an historical novel set in eighteenth-century Italy, to the nineteenth-century New York of *The House of Mirth* and later novels. In influence, Ruskin, among her early Awakeners (*Glance*, p. 67), heralds new values in *False Dawn*; and Poe, whose 'Philosophy of Furniture' is echoed in Wharton's first book, *The Decoration of Houses*,[13] leads the way through fictional dramas of the trapped consciousness such as Wharton produced early in her career, until, much later, the mature Wharton begins to treat her heroines with less restraint. In her longer fictions, Wharton moves, in other words, from Lily Barts and Anna Heaths to Charity Royalls and Halo Tarrants, just as she moves in *Old New York* from Delia Ralstons to Lizzie Hazeldeans. Complementing this movement toward liberation in subject, the collection wends its way toward liberated space, passing through drawing-rooms of constricted possibilities to reach safe havens in readers' libraries and peaceful bedrooms. It moves, in other words, away from the world of conventional restraint toward the productive spaces of a republic of the spirit—toward the libraries that were the scenes of Wharton's secret ecstasies (*Glance*, pp. 69–70) and the bedrooms from which her literary productions emerged.

Throughout her career, the author says, she wrote within the protection of her bedroom, away from the social demands placed upon the privileged hostess she never ceased to be. Considerate of her many house-guests, Wharton would emerge from her chamber to meet them for lunch, and was theirs for the rest of the day. But in the morning, before she put on the clothes of her social class, Wharton would sit in her bed, with a lap desk, and write. As Cynthia Ozick says, with Wharton 'the writing came first', first in the morning and first in her life. The bedroom and its writing board constituted, according to Ozick, 'the one uncontaminated zone of [Wharton's] being: the place unprofaned'.[14] From that place, Edith Wharton fought her good fight, telling stories in *Old New York* that old New York would not tell itself.

NOTES

1. Edith Wharton, *Old New York* (New York: Appleton, 1924) 4 vols. All references to this work will be cited parenthetically.
2. R. W. B. Lewis, *Edith Wharton: A Biography* (New York: Harper & Row Publishers, Inc., 1975) 459. All future references to this work will be cited as 'Lewis'.
3. See Blake Nevius, *Edith Wharton: A Study of her Fiction* (Berkeley, Calif.: University of California Press, 1953) on *False Dawn*; Cynthia Griffin Wolff, *A Feast of Words: The Triumph of Edith Wharton* (New York: Oxford University Press, 1977) on *The Old Maid*; and Catherine M. Rae, *Edith Wharton's New York Quartet* (Lanham, Md.: University Press of America, 1984) on a composite view.
4. See, for example, Edmund Wilson, 'Justice to Edith Wharton' repr. in *The Wound and the Bow* (Boston: Houghton Mifflin Co., 1940); Blake Nevius, op. cit.; Marilyn Jones Lyde, *Edith Wharton: Convention and Morality in the Work of a Novelist* (Norman, Okla.: University of Oklahoma Press, 1959); and Irving Howe, 'The Achievement of Edith Wharton' in *Edith Wharton: A Collection of Critical Essays*, ed. Irving Howe (Englewood Cliffs, N.J.: Prentice-Hall, 1962).
5. There have been recent departures from this dominant notion of Wharton's success in renewed looks at *Summer* (1917), *The Mother's Recompense* (1925), and *The Children* (1928), most particularly in considerations of Wharton's treatment of the theme of incest.
6. Edith Wharton, *A Backward Glance* (New York: Appleton-Century, 1934) 67–8. All future references to this work will be cited as '*Glance*'.
7. *Glance* 119. I am indebted to Martha (Ropes) Bustin, whose essay, 'Edith Wharton on Her Own Writing: A Study of Early Versions of *A Backward Glance*', ms., directed my attention to this passage.
8. Edith Wharton, *The Writing of Fiction* (New York: Charles Scribner's Sons,

1925) 18. All future references to this work will be cited as '*Fiction*'.

9. In her youth, Edith Newbold Jones completed *Fast and Loose, A Novelette by David Olivieri*, a piece of juvenalia that was published posthumously in 1977. During her lifetime, Wharton published, in addition to the novellas of *Old New York*, four other fictions that all critics agree are novellas: *The Touchstone* (1900), *Sanctuary* (1903), *Madame de Treymes* (1907), and *Bunner Sisters* (1916, though written much earlier). Wharton also published three fictions that are variously discussed as novellas or novels—*Ethan Frome* (1911), *Summer* (1917), *The Marne* (1918)—and one that is considered either a novella or a short story—"Her Son" (1933).

10. *Fiction* 44, emphasis hers. Wharton never uses the term 'novella', preferring instead, 'the long short story', 'the short novel', or, less frequently, 'the novelette'. Always, however, she uses the term '*nouvelle*' to refer to short stories. Though this brief sentence seems to hint at a theory of the novella based, for Wharton, on the treatment of subject, one can see in her discussion of *Ethan Frome* that the issue is really one of length. For a comprehensive summary of theories of the novella that touches on this key generic problem, see Charles E. May, 'The Novella' in *Critical Survey of Long Fiction*, Frank N. Magill, ed. (Englewood Cliffs, N.J.: Salem Press, 1983) 3213–339. William Dean Howells, an eminently practical man, adopted magazine parlance and spoke of the 'novella' as a one-number story, the 'novelette' as a two- or three-number story, and a 'novel' as a serial, emphasizing the scene of reception rather than the scene of production. Howells remark is cited by Fred Lewis Pattee in *The Development of the American Short Story: An Historical Survey*, (New York: Harper and Brothers, Publishers, 1923) 203. For additional consideration of terms, see Gerald Gillespie, 'Novella, Nouvelle, Novelle, Short Novel?—A Review of Terms' in *Neophilogus* 51 (1967) 117–27 and 225–30.

11. Edgar Allan Poe, 'Philosophy of Furniture' in *Selected Writings* (Middlesex: Penguin Books, 1967) 415.

12. Walt Whitman, *Leaves of Grass* in *The Portable Walt Whitman* (Middlesex: Penguin Books, 1955) 205. 'To a Common Prostitute' is part of the 1860 edition of *Leaves of Grass*, and is thus linked to the decade of *The Spark*.

13. See Judith Fryer, *Felicitous Space: The Imaginative Structures of Edith Wharton and Willa Cather* (Chapel Hill, N.C.: University of North Carolina Press, 1986) especially 95–115, for a discussion of Poe's essay in relation to *The House of Mirth*.

14. Cynthia Ozick, 'Justice Again to Edith Wharton' in *Commentary* 62 (October 1976) 57.

5

Nathanael West's 'Chamber of American Horrors'

by HAROLD BEAVER

> In the center of the principal salon was a gigantic hemorrhoid that was lit from within by electric lights. To give the effect of throbbing pain, these lights went on and off.
>
> (*A Cool Million*, Ch. 28)

Nathanael West cultivated brevity. He busied himself, sometimes for years, polishing his phrases, sentences, paragraphs. Everything needed to be as clipped and angular as a joke. Everything needed to be refined to the point of epigrammatic shock. *Miss Lonelyhearts* (1933), his one work that might normally be labelled a novella, was originally sub-titled '*A novel in the form of a comic strip*'. For it was not so much the art of the novella to which he aspired as that of the strip cartoon.

The 1920s and 1930s were the great age of the American strip cartoon. Ducks and Dumb Blondes and Dead-Eye Dicks catapulted to national fame in daily newspaper supplements of their own. West's first completed work, *The Dream Life of Balso Snell* (1931), too, was really a kind of undergraduate romp conceived in the form of a comic strip. (He had all but finished it by 1924, when he was 21, and spent the next seven years refining it.) More literate critics might call it a surrealist revue; but it was

85

surrealism transformed to a parody of the jagged jumps and colliding frames of the cartoon:

> You see me come out of the café, laughing and waving my arms.
> I hope he comes upstairs.
> You see me turn, and come towards the hotel.
> Just as soon as he comes in I'll tell him I'm pregnant. I'll tell him in a matter-of-fact voice—casually. . . .

With verbal balloons and exclamation marks exploding at the climax:

MESSENGER
> 'Beagle! Beagle! Janey has fallen from the window and is no more.'

PATRONS, WAITERS, ETC., AT THE CAFÉ CARCAS
> 'The girl you lived with is dead.'
> 'Poor Janey. Poor Beagle. Terrible, terrible death.'

A Cool Million (1934), originally sub-titled '*The Dismantling of Lemuel Pitkin*', was Horatio Alger's *Ragged Dick* condensed into a horror comic.

It was Hollywood that transformed West into the semblance of a novelist. *The Day of the Locust* (1939), his longest and most sustained work, is marked by all those movies he had scripted at the Republic studios since 1935. Its 160 scenic pages add up to rather more than a novella. Yet for all its Hollywood locations and Hollywood cast, 'The Cheated' (West's working title) were still the same old marionettes twitching on the same old showman's string. Only now their compulsions were more closely rooted in their culture. For the whole show had been visibly turned inside out. Not only the emotions and social mannerisms and verbal expressions were now fake, but the very houses, the landscape, even dreams (in the mass-production of the studios) were fake. It needed no butcher-bird, or Shrike (as in *Miss Lonelyhearts*), to hack and rend such a world. Such agonizing fakes condemned themselves. It only needed a visionary artist—a Jeremiah at its centre—to paint its self-devouring apocalypse.

That artist, Tod Hackett, was West's final incarnation. For the sad truth is that West, at the age of 37, was only just beginning to hit his stride. His literary apprenticeship was notable for an acute case of literary indigestion. Quotations from Doughty and Moore and Joyce jostle each other within paragraphs of *Balso Snell*; Swift's Lemuel Gulliver, Voltaire's Candide and Hogarth's 'Rake's Progress' compete with Kafka and the 'Horst Wessel Lied' as urtexts of *A Cool Million*. But what he was working towards was a wholly American satiric form. When ex-President Shagpoke Whipple (alias Calvin Coolidge) addresses the townsfolk of Beulah, on the Mississippi, it is the king's smalmy rhetoric (from *Huckleberry Finn*) that we overhear. Except that the lynch-mob unleashed turns against niggers, Catholics, Jews; and even that is viewed in wholly American terms. Only in America could individuals be dissolved in such irredeemable *kitsch*. 'What kind of a pretty boy was this that came apart so horribly?' asks the Maharajah in the Chinese laundryman's brothel. The answer is any American boy in the brothel that is America.

By the time he was writing *The Day of the Locust*, symbolism was kept under far tighter rein. The very title links *Exodus* (x, 12–15) to the *Book of Revelation* (ix, 3–9):

> And there came out of the smoke locusts upon the earth: and unto them was given power, as the scorpions of the earth have power . . .

> And in those days shall men seek death, and shall not find it; and shall desire to die, and death shall flee from them.

> And the shapes of the locusts were like unto horses prepared unto battle; and on their heads were as it were crowns like gold, and their faces were as the faces of men.

> And they had hair as the hair of women, and their teeth were as the teeth of lions.

> And they had breastplates, as it were breastplates of iron; and the sound of their wings was as the sound of chariots of many horses running to battle.

The thunder of these 'thousand hooves' resounds from beginning to end. That opening-shot of the Battle of Waterloo is dissolved into the punters' *Daily Running Horse*, to be transformed into Hodge's saddlery store on Sunset Boulevard where drugstore

cowboys gather to stare. Such apocalyptic horsemen gallop
from film lot to rodeo. Their meaning is death. 'Have you seen
what's in the swimming pool?' asks a guest in a Hollywood
garden, dragging Tod (meaning 'death') along a flagstone path:

> 'What is it?' he asked.
> She kicked a switch that was hidden at the base of a shrub and
> a row of submerged floodlights illuminated the green water. The
> thing was a dead horse, or, rather, a life-size, realistic repro-
> duction of one. Its legs stuck up stiff and straight and it had an
> enormous, distended belly. Its hammerhead lay twisted to one
> side and from its mouth, which was set in an agonized grin, hung
> a heavy, black tongue.
> 'Isn't it marvelous!' exclaimed Mrs. Schwartzen, clapping her
> hands and jumping up and down excitedly like a little girl.
> (*The Day of the Locust*, Ch. 4)

That twisted penis and tongue (of moulded rubber) express the
whole twisted sexuality and garrulity of that *ersatz* culture,
which is Hollywood. Even its most violent illusions are *ersatz*.

This is what had drawn West to such succinct forms in the
first place. 'In America violence is idiomatic', he had written in
1932:

> What is melodramatic in European writing is not necessarily so
> in American writing. For a European writer to make violence
> real, he has to do a great deal of careful psychology and
> sociology. He often needs three hundred pages to motivate one
> little murder. But not so the American writer. His audience has
> been prepared and is neither surprised nor shocked if he omits
> artistic excuses for familiar events.[1]

Familiarity with violence breeds violent forms. 'The short
novel', West declared, 'is a distinct form especially fitted for use
in this country.' He deplored 'the [Pearl] Bucks, [Theodore]
Dreisers and [Sinclair] Lewises'. But it was not the *novella* he
invoked so much as the *lyric novel* 'written according to Poe's
definition of a lyric poem':

> Forget the epic, the master work. In America fortunes do not
> accumulate, the soil does not grow, families have no history.
> Leave slow growth to the book reviewers, you only have time to
> explode. Remember William Carlos Williams' description of the
> pioneer women who shot their children against the wilderness
> like cannonballs. Do the same with your novels.[2]

So *Miss Lonelyhearts* moves jerkily, by fits and starts, as if crazily criss-crossing the Stations of the Cross. The sexual violence is unremitting: rape, gang bangs, arm-twisting an old fag found in an open toilet-stall. Even a Mexican war obelisk, looming 'swollen in the dying sun', looks 'as though it were about to spout a load of granite seed'. No room here for gentle dreams or tender reflections. An agony columnist, in his agony, is dismissed as 'a still more swollen Mussolini of the soul'. Only the shriek of Shrike (Miss Lonelyhearts's Grand Inquisitor) survives. Only those with 'the power to limit experience arbitrarily' can survive. As even a cripple, jerking along like 'a partially destroyed insect', survives. For it is a cripple who shoots. Mass consumption, in all its anonymity, finally takes its revenge. As the stars of Hollywood are crushed by rioting fans, here a newspaperman is inevitably felled by a gun 'wrapped in newspaper'.

Such violent antics of the text, like those of Shrike's hangers-on, are conceived as 'machines for making jokes'. That is what a gag is: a machine for making jokes. West's texts, like the Marx brothers' scripts by his brother-in-law S. J. Perelman, are criss-crossed by running gags, intended to trick and trip and disconcert the reader.[3] *The Dream Life of Balso Snell*—exhibiting Maloney the Areopagite's biography of Saint Puce, John Gilson's *Crime Journal (The Making of a Fiend)* and Miss McGeeney's *Samuel Perkins: Smeller*—is exclusively inhabited 'by writers in search of an audience'. Their scatological obsessions, in the anus of the Trojan horse, provide a stream of excremental gags—of the 'Phoenix Excrementi', of Charles Doughty's and George Moore's epigrams:

> The semites are like to a man sitting in a cloaca to the eyes, and whose brows touch heaven.

> Art is not nature, but rather nature digested. Art is sublime excrement.

Kurt Schwitters's Dada definition '*Tout ce que l'artiste crache, c'est l'art!*' (translated as 'Everything that the artist expectorates is art!') had been the original epigraph for *Balso Snell*. This was suitable enough for West's juvenilia, from what might be called his 'excrement period'. But the excremental vision was also (it is argued) 'the realistic'. Saint Puce bathing in Christ's sweat, then, purveys the very gospel of realism. T. S. Eliot's *Waste Land* becomes, quite literally, the land of waste matter, of excrement, of anal trash.[4]

That waste land is symbolically presented in the little park with the war memorial which Miss Lonelyhearts has to cross on his way to Delehanty's speakeasy:

> As far as he could discover, there were no signs of spring. The decay that covered the surface of the mottled ground was not the kind in which life generates. Last year, he remembered, May had failed to quicken these soiled fields. It had taken all the brutality of July to torture a few green spikes through the exhausted dirt.
>
> (*Miss Lonelyhearts and the dead pan*)

That generative brutality is the mark of a godless world. Miss Lonelyhearts's 'Christ complex' is absurd precisely because it is a world long ago vacated by God. Seated in the park, he searches the sky:

> But the gray sky looked as if it had been rubbed with a soiled eraser. It held no angels, flaming crosses, olive-bearing doves, wheels within wheels. Only a newspaper struggled in the air like a kite with a broken spine.

All traces of the divine have simply and brutally been excised. From his office the sky looks merely 'canvas-colored and ill-stretched':

> He examined it like a stupid detective who is searching for a clue to his own exhaustion. When he found nothing, he turned his trained eye on the skyscrapers that menaced the little park from all sides. In their tons of forced rock and tortured steel, he discovered what he thought was a clue.
>
> (*Miss Lonelyhearts on a field trip*)

It is a clue because rock-breaking and steel-making express the desperate hysteria of a civilization (summed up in Shrike) for which the 'very act of recognizing Death, Love, Beauty—all the major subjects—' had become impossible; pre-emptive judgements (mainly literary) rendered everything absurd:

> They were aware of their childishness, but did not know how else to revenge themselves. At college, and perhaps for a year afterwards, they had believed in literature, had believed in Beauty and in personal expression as an absolute end. When they lost this belief, they lost everything. (*Miss Lonelyhearts and the clean old man*)

In this meaningless world all 'is desolation and a vexation of the spirit' (in Shrike's send-up of the prophets). The cripple, dragging his days out in areaways and cellars, carries 'a heavy load of weariness and pain'. All that remains is pain. Shrike's mother-in-law with cancer of the breast, for example, dies in terrible pain. 'She died leaning over a table. The pain was so terrible that she climbed out of bed to die.' Yet even death is hard to face sincerely since 'certain precomposed judgments' (to quote John Gilson) awaited his 'method of consideration to render it absurd'.

So love too, of course, is absurd. Nuzzled by a tart, Miss Lonelyhearts merely feels 'like an empty bottle that is being slowly filled with warm, dirty water'. Following a sign 'To Kamp Komfit' on the film lot, Tod Hackett merely reaches 'a Greek temple dedicated to Eros. The god himself lay face downward in a pile of old newspapers and bottles.' Love, death, beauty—everything is turned to junk, to waste, to excrement in this god-forsaken universe.

No wonder Miss Lonelyhearts, Lemuel Pitkin, Tod Hackett—all West's major protagonists—feel impotent. They prove impotent in a universe implacably resistant to their dreams. Yet it is precisely their dreams that make them so vulnerable in the first place to a society where only con-men triumph, con-men to whom they instinctively feel drawn (that is the joke) in their longing for some more active participation and rôle. The result is invariably that tragic clowning, that burlesque of feeling, that bitter laugh at laughter itself which the young West located in *Hamlet*, in Dostoevsky, in Chekhov, Kafka, Kurt Schwitters—everywhere but the bulky epics of 'the Bucks, Dreisers and Lewises'. Only Twain in earlier American literature, it seems, had anything to offer.

Like most of the rest of his generation, he could blame the Great War:

> Having no alternative, Balso blamed the war, the invention of printing, nineteen-century science, communism, the wearing of soft hats, the use of contraceptives, the large number of delica-tessen stores, the movies, the tabloids, the lack of adequate ventilation in large cities, the passing of the saloon, the soft collar fad, the spread of foreign art, the decline of the western world, commercialism, and, finally, for throwing the artist back on his own personality, the renaissance.

That absurdly itemized list was also to become a hallmark of West's style. He could shuffle and reshuffle his heterogeneous pack without discovering a clue to hierarchy or order. 'Like children at their game,' wrote Kierkegaard, 'the ironist counts on his fingers: rich man, poor man, beggar man, etc.' He continues:

> All those incarnations only represent for him pure potentialities, so that he can run their gamut as fast as children playing their game. . . . If reality thus loses its value in the ironist's eyes, it is not because it has been outgrown and must make room for a more authentic reality, but because the ironist embodies the 'fundamental I' to which there is no corresponding reality.[5]

West never found that corresponding reality, only 'a dream-like violence'. In New York Miss Lonelyhearts studies the people's 'broken hands and torn mouths' with an overwhelming desire (mingled with guilt) to help them. In Los Angeles the crowd turns demoniac:

> Once there, they discover that sunshine isn't enough. They get tired of oranges, even of avocado pears and passion fruit. Nothing happens. They don't know what to do with their time. They haven't the mental equipment for leisure, the money nor the physical equipment for pleasure. Did they slave so long just to go to an occasional Iowa picnic? What else is there? They watch the waves come in at Venice. There wasn't any ocean where most of them came from, but after you've seen one wave, you've seen them all. The same is true of the airplanes at Glendale. If only a plane would crash once in a while so that they could watch the passengers being consumed in a 'holocaust of flame', as the newspapers put it.
>
> (*The Day of the Locust*, Ch. 27)

Some try cock-fighting to evade that mindless, intolerable boredom. Others feed on newspapers or just go to the movies to feed 'on lynchings, murder, sex crimes, explosions, wrecks, love nests, fires, miracles, revolutions, war. . . . Nothing can ever be violent enough to make taut their slack minds and bodies'. For Tod Hackett, as for all his predecessors, there is no evading that boredom: no escape in religion or art or even the South Sea Islands. There was no 'corresponding reality' to man's deepest, most idiosyncratic instincts. Better far to dream of returning to the womb, or cry with Job:

Why died I not from the womb? why did I not give up the ghost
when I came out of the belly?

Why did the knees prevent me? or why the breasts that I should
suck?

For now should I have lain still and been quiet, I should have
slept: then had I been at rest.

(iii, 11–13)

West, like a latterday Job, admits no comforters.

This culture, then, can only be grasped through its prolifera-
tion of signs. Being wholly without mystery or meaning, its
articulation proves nothing but a circulation of signs. For they
necessarily shift and drift. Unanchored, they confound their
paradigms in reckless substitutions. On Hollywood's Vine
Street, for example:

> great many of the people wore sports clothes which were not
> really sports clothes. Their sweaters, knickers, slacks, blue
> flannel jackets with brass buttons were fancy dress. The fat lady
> in the yachting cap was going shopping, not boating; the man in
> the Norfolk jacket and Tyrolean hat was returning, not from a
> mountain, but an insurance office; and the girl in slacks and
> sneaks with a bandanna around her head had just left a switch-
> board, not a tennis court.
>
> (*The Day of the Locust*, Ch. 1)

Their houses, too, are exact stylistic reproductions of other
houses, whose owners in their turn impersonate their owners, so
that a Chinese servant is turned into a black, a Scotch and soda
into a 'mint julep', and a slip of a man rocks to and fro on his
'colonial' porch masquerading as a large-bellied Southern
colonel. Styles float as signs float. There is a confusion of signals
as *signifiant* (in Saussure's terms) is everywhere divorced from
signifié. Gumwood is painted to resemble fumed oak. Machine-
made hinges are carefully stamped to appear hand-forged.
Heavy fireproof paper for thatching is coloured and ribbed to
look like straw. But instead of revelling in this riot of in-
determinate and promiscuous signs—as Barthes in that *'empire
des signes'* he called Japan—West indicts the confusion.[6]
Nothing is what it seems. Everything in Hollywood is fake—the
clothes, the gestures, the religion; even a corpse is faked by the

undertakers to look 'like the interlocutor in a minstrel show'.

This is a society consumed by its own clichés, just as the text of *Balso Snell* had been consumed by the platitudes of its own rhetoric.[7] In enacting those clichés, it becomes them; but since they are meaningless, each is interchangeable at whim. In *Miss Lonelyhearts* characters were reduced to mere labels: 'Desperate', 'Broken-hearted', 'Sick-of-it-all'. Or they were transformed to fleeting reflections of the texts around them. In a restaurant, called El Gaucho, a woman 'immediately went Spanish and her movements became languorous and full of abandon'. On reaching the outskirts of New York, another 'began to act like an excited child, greeting the trees and grass with delight'. Miss Lonelyhearts, in his confusion, actually proposed to a 'party dress':

> He begged the party dress to marry him, saying all the things it expected to hear, all the things that went with strawberry sodas and farms in Connecticut. He was just what the party dress wanted him to be: simple and sweet, whimsical and poetic, a trifle collegiate yet very masculine.
>
> (*Miss Lonelyhearts and the party dress*)

In *The Day of the Locust* the characters are less fluid, though equally confused. Now they are ventriloquists' dummies, rather: out of vaudeville routines (Harry Greener), Hollywood revues (Faye Greener), or rodeo shows (Earle Shoop).

Still the signs do not match. Signal and message do not seem to correspond. It is not just the faking that is evident, but the slippage, the utter dissociation between *any* language and *any* meaning. Faye Greener's elaborate gestures are 'so completely meaningless, almost formal' that she seems a dancer rather than an affected actress. That is what attracts Tod Hackett. It is this ballerina body-language—so purified of meaning, so aesthetically formal—that speaks to the artist in Tod:

> The strange thing about her gestures and expressions was that they didn't really illustrate what she was saying. They were almost pure. It was as though her body recognized how foolish her words were and tried to excite her hearers into being uncritical.
>
> (*The Day of the Locust*, Ch. 22)

She is not unique. Even a landlady's fascination with funerals, it turns out, 'wasn't morbid; it was formal. She was interested in the arrangement of the flowers, the order of the procession, the clothing and deportment of the mourners' (*The Day of the Locust*, Ch. 16). Such pantomime 'of formal, impersonal gestures'— gestures at once 'too appropriate' and inappropriate—is the consistent trade-mark of West's style.

All rôles are rôle-playing. Like Harry Greener's music-hall charades, like Shrike's 'little nods and winks', they are masks covering masks—'nothing but surface stratified on surface' (in Melville's phrase),[8] or onions (in Barthes's image) constructed of layers, or levels, or systems, whose body contains finally no heart, no kernel, no secret, no irreducible principle. So all are dispensable and interchangeable and replaceable. All are equally discards (like the letter-writers of *Miss Lonelyhearts*), throw-away commodities of a throw-away culture. A dwarf is initially mistaken for 'a pile of soiled laundry'. A cowboy's 'two-dimensional face' might have been drawn by a talented child with a ruler and compass. Harry Greener snaps, at the first heart-attack, like a worn out automaton:

> Suddenly, like a mechanical toy that had been overwound, something snapped inside of him and he began to spin through his entire repertoire. The effort was purely muscular, like the dance of a paralytic. He jigged, juggled his hat, made believe he had been kicked, tripped, and shook hands with himself. He went through it all in one dizzy spasm, then reeled to the couch and collapsed.
>
> (*The Day of the Locust*, Ch. 11)

That is the terrifying vision behind West's farce. These characters are not merely emotionally twisted or physically deformed (like Sherwood Anderson's 'grotesques'), they are shoddy. They are trash. They are waste products to be junked like used razor blades in the Grand Canyon, or to be dumped on that 'final dumping ground', the 'dream dump' of Hollywood.

Nathanael West wrote not 'novellas' so much as Menippean farces to shock America out of its mass-produced and mass-consumed formulaic expectations. To quote *Balso Snell*:

> In case the audience should misunderstand and align itself on the side of the artist, the ceiling of the theatre will be made to open and cover the occupants with tons of loose excrement. After the deluge, if they so desire, the patrons of my art can gather in the customary charming groups and discuss the play.

NOTES

1. West, 'Some Notes on Violence', *Contact*, Vol. 1, No. 3 (1932), 132–33; reprinted in Nathanael West, *A Collection of Critical Essays*, ed. Jay Martin (Englewood Cliffs, N.J.: Prentice-Hall, 1971).
2. West, 'Some Notes on Miss L.', *Contempo*, Vol. 3 (15 May 1933), 1–2 (reprinted in Martin (ed.), *Critical Essays*).
3. Compare *The Dream Life of Balso Snell* with S. J. Perelman's merry spin, *Through the Fallopian Tubes on a Bicycle*, later published as *Parlor, Bedlam and Bath* (New York: H. Liveright, 1930).
4. Cf. Warwick Wadlington: 'The polluting detritus of a civilization, rather than its barrenness, is the emphasis, sharply reversing the order of stress in Eliot's famous piece' (*The Confidence Game in American Literature* (Princeton University Press, 1975), Pt. 3, Ch. 9, p. 296).
5. Kierkegaard, *The Concept of Irony*, quoted by Gilles Deleuze, *Logique du sens* (Paris: Éditions de Minuit, 1969), pp. 164–65.
6. In Japan, according to Barthes, 'the empire of signifiers is so vast, so far in excess of speech, that the exchange of signs constitutes a density, a mobility, a subtlety, which is spell-binding' (*L'Empire des signes* (Geneva, 1970), pp. 18–20).
7. Cf. Jonathan Raban, 'A Surfeit of Commodities: The Novels of Nathanael West', in *The American Novel and the Nineteen Twenties*, ed. Malcolm Bradbury and David Palmer, (London: Edward Arnold, 1971), pp. 215–31.
8. Melville: '. . . found to consist of nothing but surface stratified on surface. To its axis, the world being nothing but superinduced superficies' (*Pierre; or, The Ambiguities* (1852; Evanston and Chicago: Newberry Library, 1971), pp. 284–85).

6

Contrasts in Form: Hemingway's *The Old Man and the Sea* and Faulkner's 'The Bear'[1]

by DAVID TIMMS

1

It is paradoxical that while most of us feel diffident about formulating definitions of the novel, we are confident about which texts we wish to call 'novels'. No wonder we are reluctant to offer definitions. The novel's bastard nature was acknowledged early: *Joseph Andrews* is famously a 'comic epic poem in prose'. That the novel is 'mimetic' or tends towards the 'referential' would be an area of agreement even for critics of widely divergent aesthetics: Erich Auerbach and Roman Jakobson perhaps.[2] But the very fact that the world comes so insistently into the form makes it more obviously the ground for contesting ideologies. This suggests that it is impossible to make a list of necessary qualities we would all agree on. Even Forster's unfashionably unambitious definition, that the novel is 'any fictitious prose work over 50,000 words,'[3] has been contradicted by Nabokov's *Pale Fire*, which opens with a substantial verse section. But it seems that as readers we find it easy to recognize 'family resemblances' between novels. Texts as different as *Tristram Shandy* and *Middlemarch* are clearly

97

siblings, but *Gulliver's Travels* is equally clearly only a cousin.

But oddly, the opposite seems to apply with regard to the novella. Here, we can find defining characteristics. Length is the most obvious. Mary Doyle Springer in *Forms of the Modern Novella* (1975) refines Forster when she says that the novella is 'a prose fiction of a certain length (usually 15,000 to 50,000 words)'.[4] That is fair enough: novellas are that length, otherwise they are short stories or novels. But what about ascribing particular works to the class of novellas? James's 'The Death of the Lion' seems unproblematically a novella, especially since he gives his own *imprimatur* to the description.[5] But 'The Aspern Papers' or 'The Turn of the Screw'? They are both within the word-limit. Conrad provides a more striking instance. I would call *The Nigger of the 'Narcissus'* a novella, but not *Heart of Darkness*.

These examples hint that the difference may be one of value, and indeed that distinction has been offered by plausible voices. F. R. Leavis, for instance, jibbed at the word '*nouvelle*' for Lawrence's *St. Mawr*: 'that description, with its limiting effect, has a marked infelicity. It certainly doesn't suggest the nature or weight of the astonishing work of genius that Lawrence's "dramatic poem" is.'[6] Nabokov is thinking in similar categories when he suggests dismissively that the writer of novellas operates by 'diminishing large things and enlarging small ones'.[7] James on the other hand would not have accepted this conflation of 'novella' and 'novelette'; he referred to the *nouvelle* as a 'blest' form.[8]

Certainly a qualitative distinction will not do to separate *The Old Man and the Sea* and 'The Bear' either from other prose fictions or from each other. In a most useful examination of the history of the term 'novella' Gerald Gillespie includes both works as distinguished modern examples of the form:

> William Faulkner's 'The Bear' is still very close to the 'simple' *novella*, to Hemingway's 'Old Man and The Sea', because it demonstrates through the creature hunted and the participants of the hunt a natural order that becomes visible precisely in the confrontation with the particular symbol.[9]

This seems to me to raise exactly the kind of problem I refer to above. While Gillespie's general comments on the nature of the novella are unobjectionable, this particular ascription of texts seems to me unsatisfactory. I hope an explanation of that unsatisfactoriness might be suggestive not only about the texts themselves, but also about the nature of the novella.

2

It is evident at the outset that *The Old Man and the Sea* and 'The Bear' have similarities beyond their roughly equal length. Gillespie's brief description of the thematic content of the two texts places them both in a tradition of American fictions that begins as early as Cooper's *The Pioneers* (1823) and has been expressed in both 'high' and 'low' culture ever since. Michael Cimino's *The Deer Hunter* (1978) is a recent example. The tradition tells the story of a man's confronting nature and expressing in the confrontation elements of nobility that match what he confronts, and contrast with the society that surrounds him outside the forest or on shore. It is a theme characteristically American, in more than one sense, as 'The Bear' makes clear:

> There was always a bottle present, so that it would seem to him that those fierce fine instants of heart and brain and courage and wiliness and speed were concentrated and distilled into that brown liquor which not women, not boys and children, but only hunters drank, drinking not of the blood they spilled but some condensation of the wild immortal spirit, drinking it moderately, humbly even, not with the pagan's base and baseless hope of acquiring thereby the virtues of cunning and strength and speed but in salute to them. Thus it seemed to him on this December morning not only natural but actually fitting that this should have begun with whisky.[10]

This view of the hunter is very specific. As the text points out, it is not at all 'pagan', and that is confirmed in anthropological works. According to James W. Fernandez, the 'Fang', a people of western equatorial Africa, use metaphors that make an analogy between men good at hunting and men who are good judges generally. He suggests that this is straightforward common sense and economic hard-headedness: 'Everyone knows the difference between a good and a bad hunter. The evidence comes home in his bag.'[11] But in 'The Bear', though it is a measure of Boon Hogganbeck's inferiority that he is in a position to shoot the bear and misses, it is a measure of Ike McCaslin's superiority and worthiness that he is in a position to shoot the bear and won't. While Santiago in Hemingway's story does kill the fish, he is like McCaslin above the concerns of cash. He does not get it home, and even though the meat would have brought him a great deal of money, his concern that the sharks have 'ruined' the marlin has nothing to do with economics. It is not even that being a 'hunter' carries a mark of social distinction, as it does in Britain. In both texts being a hunter is like being a priest.

If this is a characteristically American view it is also characteristically male. Richard Poirier commends Faulkner's careful balance of negatives in this very passage from 'The Bear' and tries to tell us that 'the description of things being dismissed by the negatives is never foreshortened or contemptuous.'[12] Could he really make that assertion if he read 'as a woman' the bracketing of their sex with boys and children? Simone de Beauvoir in *The Second Sex* (1949) suggests that in a patriarchal culture hunting is the initial source of male status: superiority 'has been accorded in humanity not to the sex that brings forth but to that which kills'.[13] Faulkner is not even that positive here: the real force of the negatives is that 'hunter' equals 'minus female'. His drink is defined as that which women do *not* drink. The hunters do not use sheets but sleep under blankets, whose 'rough male kiss' Rupert Brooke noticed in another context. They have no interest in the virtues of good cooking, traditionally defined (at least in its domestic context) with women. Bizarrely, given his appearance, the figure of Boon Hogganbeck underlines this devaluation: within the symbolism of the text, he is female. The dog Lion 'don't care about nothing or nobody', but Boon 'knelt beside him, feeling the bones and muscles, the power. It was as if Lion were a woman—or perhaps Boon was the woman. That was more like it . . .' (167). We should not be surprised then to find he does not drink reverentially but immoderately, and cannot shoot straight. He stresses his alliance with the non-hunters in the final words of the book: he lays claim to the squirrels ('They're mine') when 'proven hunters . . . scorned such' (155).

Though women appear only as concepts in the central experiences of 'The Bear' and *The Old Man and the Sea*, what might be called 'the Female' is everywhere. Nina Baym identifies a recurrent pattern in 'the' American tradition:

> . . . the rôle of the beckoning wilderness, the attractive landscape, is given a deeply feminine quality. Landscape is deeply imbued with female qualities, as society is: but where society is menacing and destructive, landscape is compliant and supportive. It has the attributes simultaneously of a virginal bride and a non-threatening mother; its female qualities are articulated with respect to a male angle of vision: what can nature do for me, asks the hero, what can it give me?[14]

These precise female identifications are not entirely accurate for 'The Bear' or *The Old Man and the Sea*, but in both cases, landscape is seen as female, inviting and sexually compliant:

> [Santiago] always thought of the sea as *la mar* which is what people call her in Spanish when they love her . . . the old man always thought of her as feminine and as something that gave or withheld great favours, and if she did wild or wicked things it was because she could not help them. The moon affects her as it does a woman, he thought.[15]

For Ike McCaslin, what he experiences in the woods is 'the existence of love and passion and experience which is his heritage and not yet his patrimony', and the taste of it is the same as when 'entering by chance the presence or perhaps even merely the bedroom of a woman who has loved and been loved by many men' (155). This world is properly at the disposition of the genuine male principle. Old Ben is called colloquially 'the head bear . . . the man' (150) by Sam, his votary, and the maleness of the great swordfish is grossly Freudian. In this world the 'natural' order of male over female is rigidly maintained: Ben rakes the shoulder of the bitch who dares to look at him; only a male dog is able to hold him. The lords of the landscape are distinguished by a superior indifference to the female of their own species: both Ben and the great marlin are solitary, and their single state is imitated by their accolytes.

Not so in the social world ever closing in on Santiago and McCaslin. It is the world of commerce and industry, lumber factories, locomotives and fish-canneries, and its voice is feminine. From his relationship with the bear and Sam Fathers, Ike learns that he must 'repudiate' the legacy of 'his' land, because the whole notion of 'ownership' of the land is tainted. But his wife tempts him with sexual favours to repossess it, and withdraws them when he refuses. In *The Old Man and the Sea*, too, a woman speaks for society when she sees the skeleton of the marlin on the beach among the 'empty beer cans and dead barracudas'. She asks a waiter what it is and the waiter offers 'Tiburon . . . Eshark' in explanation of what happened to the great fish. She misunderstands, and thinks that she is looking at the skeleton of what the book has taught us to associate with what is sneaking and evil:

> 'I didn't know sharks had such handsome, beautifully formed tails.'
> 'I didn't either,' her male companion said. (109)

For a double reason women cannot be *aficionados*, and besides getting the facts wrong, the woman here diminishes what the reader is supposed to have experienced as a struggle of tragic proportions to a question of aesthetics. She reduces the 'value' of the fish as surely as the sharks did. Both texts conform to a definition offered by Judith Fetterley: 'To be American is male; and the quintessential American experience is betrayal by a woman.'[16]

Annette Kolodny has reminded us that a view of the landscape as female and compliant is anything but 'natural' if you are yourself a woman, and she has also stressed that the verbal appropriation of the landscape by men was matched by its physical appropriation, from which women were largely excluded.[17] Given this exclusion, if 'The Bear' yet again excuses Adam and blames 'the woman' for the fall from grace, it must be hypocritical . . . but does it, at least in simple terms?

In *History, Ideology and Myth in American Fiction, 1823–1852* (1984) Richard Clark has suggested that 'the' American tradition shown to be a construct by recent feminist critics might be seen to have a more particular ideological function than simply to affirm patriarchy. He schematizes the form of the characteristic myth retold by texts in this tradition as 'Civilisation threatens Adamic Innocent living in harmony with Edenic Nature.'[18] It cloaks the actuality, which was an attempt to make 'Eden' economically profitable. The myth has a relationship with history rather like the relationship of dream and reality in

Freudian theory: it can represent actual situations 'the other way round', with the purpose of providing 'a wish-fulfilling image of man's relationship with nature'.

> Where in historical reality we know that blacks and Indians were exploited and expropriated by the whites, in the mythic representation we are offered the famous couples—Natty and Chingachgook, Ishmael and Queequeg, Huck and Nigger Jim—in which the innocent white man is symbolically allied with his victim in opposition to the advance of white civilisation. Evidently the figure of the white innocent has been produced by condensation and displacement of both material and ideological elements and can be interpreted as acting either as a denial of real conditions . . . or as a recuperation of them.[19]

If this operates for blacks and Indians, it also operates for women in both *The Old Man and the Sea* and 'The Bear', at least in my representation of it so far. But that representation is limited, and this simplified statement of myth does not hold good for Faulkner's story as a whole. 'Civilisation' in the shape of old Carrothers McCaslin predates the Adamic Innocent. Ike McCaslin overtly confronts precisely those historical facts Clark identifies, but while Ike has moral stature at some points of the story, at others he seems ludicrous and his ideals naïf. The woods do indeed have their noble prelapsarian aspect, and Old Ben is an expression of it; but the Garden also already contains the serpent whom Ike calls 'Grandfather' near the end of the work (251). The complex represented by 'The Bear' will not conform with Clark's scheme, except in a way that is so partial as to raise more questions than it answers. On the other hand, there are no such complications in *The Old Man and the Sea*. It has one digression, in the shape of the episode of Santiago's arm-wrestling with the huge black. This digression however does not obscure the issue but clarifies it, since it functions in a straightforwardly allegorical way to the main story.

I suggest that it is on the complications of 'The Bear' and in the antithetical singleness and clarity of *The Old Man and the Sea* that the satisfactoriness or otherwise of the description 'novella' depends. Todorov suggests that 'there is no time, in reading a short work, to forget it is only "literature" and not "life" '[20]; but the novel classically encourages us 'to find Swann's/ Way better than our own', as Randall Jarrell put it.[21] Though the two texts are alike as to length, *The Old Man and the Sea* follows the aesthetic principle the novella's brevity hints at, while 'The Bear' does not.

3

Definitions of the novella must take into account its most eloquent modern apologist, Henry James, and the suggestions about the form in his prefaces offer what he himself would probably have called a *point d'appui*. In connection with 'The Death of the Lion' he recalls the relief with which he greeted his editor's advice that he need not confine himself to the 'six to eight thousand words' usual in periodical publication:

> Among forms, moreover, we had had, on the dimensional ground—for length and breadth—our ideal, the beautiful and blest *nouvelle*; the generous, the enlightened hour for which appeared thus at last to shine. . . . For myself I delighted in the shapely *nouvelle*—as, for that matter, I had from time to time here and there been almost encouraged to show.[22]

I should like to concentrate on the two features James picks out: length and shapeliness.

Many critics, following Lukacs, have suggested that the novel uniquely gives the sense of lives shaped not simply by events but by the passage of time itself. This is not to say that all novels do, of course, but those which do not seem conspicuous in not doing so. In an essay on this topic Eleanor Hutchens notes that such novels 'make up the body of the anti-novelistic novel.'[23] That is not to say that the events in novellas do not sometimes take place over long periods of time: 'The Beast in the Jungle' is a case in point. But novellas differ from novels in that they do not give a sense of the experience of the passing of time. They will pick out only significant moments. In the novel, it is the very inclusion of events of lesser significance, of periods of time with no highlights, that gives the sense of time passing. The line of least resistance for the novella is to do as Hemingway's does, and confine action to a short period, in the case of *The Old Man and the Sea* some three days and nights. 'The Bear' is quite different in this respect. At different points of the narrative Ike appears as a small boy and as an old man, 'uncle to half a country and father to none' (228). Look for instance at this comment on his gun:

> He had his own gun now, a new breech-loader, a Christmas gift; he would own and shoot it through two new pairs of barrels and one new stock, until all that remained of the original gun was the silver-inlaid trigger-guard with his and McCaslin's engraved names and the date in 1878. (156)

The focus is on Ike's central experience with the bear, but passages like this encourage us to do what Eleanor Hutchens notes of reading novels, even those with central figures like Clarissa Dalloway or Leopold Bloom: we put one event always in the context of another, reconstruct a whole life in the experience of reading.

Analogous to the inclusion of 'inessential' events in plots of novels is the inclusion of 'superfluous' detail in describing settings. Such details function by virtue of their very irrelevance; as Barthes notes, it reminds us of the contingency of life and therefore testifies to the 'reality' of the world the novel represents.[24] On this point 'The Bear' and *The Old Man and the Sea* diverge once more. Events in 'The Bear' take place in many locations besides the woods, and of all of them we are given some physical sense. Of course the whole situation of Santiago— he is far out at sea and is materially impoverished anyway—is one that admits of little in the way of physical description, but then that is my point: the novella is well-adapted to such narrow settings.

The same is true of character, partly in simple quantitative terms: the novella finds it hard to accommodate a large cast. *The Old Man and the Sea* abides by the suggestions of the form in having only two major parts (the fish and the man), one supporting actor (Manolin), and a few bit-parts. 'The Bear' on the other hand has not only two star rôles (Ike and McCaslin) but two large animal parts as well, and one for a good supporting small dog. There are a number of important 'character' parts (Boon, Sam Fathers, Major de Spain, Ash, the educated black), an opportunity to introduce a starlet, and a large cast of extras. There is a difference qualitatively, too, for the form surely does not encourage psychological complexity. Where an individual's psychology is the subject (as in 'The Beast in the Jungle' once more) the tendency is to treat a single issue. *The Old Man and the Sea* obeys this principle and is not 'psychological', the emphasis being on what the old man does, rather than on what he thinks: on the moral status rather than the springs of his actions. A great deal of 'The Bear' is given over to Ike's motives, and attention is paid to the way in which a whole range of events shape his psyche. Perhaps I should say 'happenings', for Ike is a very passive hero, especially in contrast with Santiago. 'The Beast in the Jungle' comes once more to mind; Ike is more like one of James's heroes than one of Hemingway's.

The Old Man and the Sea deals with a single theme: the possibility of creating significance through dignity and courage in a natural and social world devoid of inherent meanings. The marlin's world is full of sharks; the old man's world is full of people like Manolin's parents who put cash reward above loyalty, or the woman tourist who cannot tell an ignoble fish from a noble one. Gerald Gillespie traces the lineage of the novella from the Latin *exemplum*, and notes the contribution of the Italian *novellino*, the little anecdote that has a moral.[25] Erich Auerbach, too, notes that the *novellino* has the form of an *exemplum*, and comments that the style is 'flatly paratactic . . . with the events strung together as though on a thread, without palpable breadth and without an atmosphere for the characters to breathe in'.[26] The dismissive tone apart, this seems to me an adequate description of *The Old Man and the Sea* in terms of style, plot and setting. But it is surely appropriate to present such a theme in paratactic language and by means of a paratactic plot: this is a world without a teleology or even an eschatology, where the only inherent organizing principle or end product is blank sequence. The only way to make such a world meaningful is to force life and death into a context of your own manufacture where they are not arbitrary; for Santiago the assumed moral imperatives of a ritual contest between his own cunning and experience and the fish's strength. In a well-known letter to H. G. Wells, James expressed something similar: 'it is art that *makes* life . . . makes importance.'[27] But as Walter Benjamin stresses, in the 'story' (and he explicitly includes the novella in this category), '*one* hero, *one* odyssey, *one* battle',[28] and in *The Old Man and the Sea* this singleness is evident in language and narrative style.

Once more 'The Bear' is quite different. It includes a variation on Hemingway's single theme, but Faulkner has ancilliary themes that have a more or less independent existence. The race issue, for instance, branches in several different directions. It is not simply another instance of the damage wreaked by the original sin of presuming to own land and buy and sell it. 'The Bear' deals with the issue of the exploitation of female slaves, and the right to inheritance of the black descendants of slave-owners. It deals with the usefulness or otherwise of 'educating' blacks without giving them proper means of subsistence. It deals with the distinctive qualities of blacks as a racial group, and refers to the different stresses of having black and Indian, or white and Indian ancestry.

If the style of *The Old Man and the Sea* is consonant with its single theme, that of 'The Bear' is appropriate for its complex and multiple ones:

> And He probably knew it was vain but He had created them, and he knew them capable of all things because He had shaped them out of the Primal Absolute which contained all and had watched them since in their individual exaltation and baseness and they themselves not knowing why nor how nor even when: until at last He saw that they were all Grandfather all of them and that even from them the elected and chosen the best the very best He could expect (not hope mind: not hope) would be Bucks and Buddies and not even enough of them. (215–16)

The language here is hypotactic and grammatically embedded. Ike's wish to find exactly the right word, which goes to the extent of referring to the near relatives that will not do ('not hope mind: not hope'), paradoxically makes the semantics more obscure. The whole, content and style, encourages the reader to see Ike McCaslin's life and problems as complex and confusing— and indeed it is one of Ike's failings that he does not recognize this himself, believing that the simple act of renouncing his land will restore the Garden to order.

This complexity is enormously increased by the fact that 'The Bear' does not maintain a single angle of vision or attitude towards its themes and characters, as *The Old Man and the Sea* does. The attitude the latter wishes to encourage in its reader is like Manolin's at the end: a sort of sad, admiring resignation. It is made bitter-sweet by the introduction of the woman tourist, a member of a crass out-group that serves to define the membership of the sensitive in-group: Santiago, Manolin, narrator and reader. Once more 'The Bear' is very different. While Santiago is not a conventional hero he is consistently heroic and is never presented in a light that will show him as either mean or laughable. He belongs in a tradition of 'naturally noble' American fictional heroes that goes back at least to Natty Bumppo. But Ike McCaslin's naïvety is often laughable, and he does not even have the dignified simplicity of a Huck Finn, say. This is clear from his cousin's antiphonal responses when Ike catalogues black virtues:

> 'They are better than we are, stronger than we are. . . . Their vices are aped from white men. . . .'
> 'All right. Go on: promiscuity. Violence. Instability and lack of control. Inability to distinguish between mine and thine—' and he
> 'How distinguish, when for two hundred years mine did not even exist for them?' and McCaslin
> 'All right. Go on. And their virtues—' and he
> 'Yes. Their own. Endurance—' and McCaslin
> 'So have mules:' and he
> '—and pity and tolerance and forebearance and fidelity and love of children—' and McCaslin
> 'So have dogs.' (225)

Ike's tone here is too righteous and too humble for us to be convinced that the text is wholly behind him; McCaslin as the voice of the common man is too tart and too humorous for the reader simply to dismiss him as a self-interested cynic.

The grandness of Ike's renunciation has a comic and even farcical corrective in the story of Uncle Hubert's bequest. Ike's indigent uncle had nobly promised to leave his nephew a silver cup full of gold coins, which he ceremoniously sealed in a burlap package before the whole family. Over the years, Ike had noticed unaccounted-for changes in the shape of the package, and in its sound when rattled. He discovers the reason for the alterations only when the burlap is unsealed on his twenty-first birthday. Uncle Hubert had 'borrowed' the gold coins one by one, and replaced them with I.O.U.s. Finally he had exchanged the precious cup for a tin coffee-pot. Romance has turned to broad humour, but humour itself turns to irony when Ike pragmatically finds the coffee-pot useful: the silver cup would have been merely ornamental. Something similar happens on a more local level when McCaslin asks Ike why he did not shoot the bear when he had the chance. It is a serious topic, and Ike replies seriously by quoting Keats's 'Ode on a Grecian Urn', implying something like 'Heard melodies are sweet, but those unheard/ Are sweeter.' But can this reference remain serious in the context of Uncle Hubert's silver cup, or when we remember that Keats's poem is partly about a man not catching a young woman, when Ike is obsessed with his Grandfather's catching them too often?

Robert Scholes's contribution to a most useful collection of essays, *Towards a Poetics of Fiction* (1977), proposes a diagram that classifies fictions by genre.[29] He gives us a diagram based on an inverted triangle.

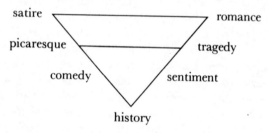

Any fiction can be placed relative to others somewhere in the triangle. Fictions that represent life as it actually is are 'histories', and others vary according to whether they tend to represent life as being better than it is (romance) or worse than it is (satire). Traditional 'novels' are all placed within the bottom two-thirds of the diagram, below a line drawn between picaresque and tragedy. They are mixtures: indeed the fact that they are mixtures is constitutive of their being novels. Where would *The Old Man and the Sea* and 'The Bear' fit? In different places, I suggest. I would place *The Old Man and the Sea* above the picaresque-tragedy line, near tragedy rather than romance. The position of 'The Bear' is more problematic, but certainly it would be below the line, not above. It is drawn down towards 'history' by its complex plot and characterization and its multiple themes, and by its seeing them in both comic and tragic lights: by its seeing life mimetically, 'as it is', in fact.

Novellas as a class would not simply occupy a zone within the area taken up by novels as a whole in Scholes's triangle. Many of the most characteristic would fall outside that area, whether they tend towards satire on the one hand, or towards romance on the other. Another and more famous geometric metaphor for fiction is the circle from James's preface to *Roderick Hudson*:

> Really, universally, relations stop nowhere, and the exquisite problem of the artist is eternally but to draw, by a geometry of his own, the circle within which they shall happily *appear* to do so.[30]

While James's formulation is a just one, it must also be said that the firmer the circle is drawn, the less will be the sense of the multifariousness of life; the more heterogeneous the world included, the less clear will the outline of the circle be, if the shape is maintained at all. The novella is surely a form that stresses the circle, both by the obvious measure of length, and by the less obvious measure of 'shapeliness'. To that extent it gives less of the sense of heterogeneousness that is characteristic of the novel form. I hesitate to offer a reductive definition, but what seems to be the case is that the novella is a form that operates within a narrower technical and thematic range, and that this influences its generic possibilities. Brevity encourages this limitation of techniques, themes and generic possibilities rather than enforces it; but it is precisely when a fiction of novella length adopts heterogeneous technical, thematic and genre features that we become unhappy with the description 'novella'. By this measure, *The Old Man and the Sea* is a model novella, and while I have had no intention of trusting the teller rather than the tale, I am glad not to have to go against Faulkner himself, who had the sub-title of *Go Down, Moses and Other Stories* removed from its second printing.[31]

NOTES

1. *The Old Man and the Sea* was first printed as a separate volume (1952), but 'The Bear' first appeared as the longest of a group of interconnected stories in *Go Down, Moses* (1942). While both texts have appeared in a

variety of contexts since first publication, I have adhered to the convention suggested by the original appearance in italicizing the title of Hemingway's narrative, and putting Faulkner's in inverted commas.

2. Erich Auerbach, *Mimesis: The Representation of Reality in Western Literature* (1946), trans. Willard R. Trask (Princeton: Princeton University Press, 1963); Roman Jakobson, 'Closing Statement: Linguistics and Poetics', in T. Sebeok (ed.), *Style in Language* (Cambridge, Mass.: M.I.T. Press, 1960), pp. 350–70.

3. E. M. Forster, *Aspects of the Novel* (1927; Harmondsworth: Penguin Books, 1962), pp. 13–14.

4. Mary Doyle Springer, *Forms of the Modern Novella* (Chicago and London: University of Chicago Press, 1975), p. 93.

5. *The Art of the Novel: Critical Prefaces by Henry James*, ed. R. P. Blackmur (New York: Charles Scribner's Sons, 1934), p. 220.

6. F. R. Leavis, 'The Novel as Dramatic Poem: *St. Mawr*', (1950) rpt. in Stephen Hazell (ed.), *The English Novel: Developments in Criticism since Henry James* (London: Macmillan, 1978), p. 85.

7. Quoted in Springer, p. 5.

8. *The Art of the Novel*, p. 220.

9. Gerald Gillespie, 'Novella, Nouvelle, Novelle, Short Novel? A Review of Terms', *Neophilologus*, 51 (1967), 227.

10. William Faulkner, 'The Bear', in *Go Down, Moses and Other Stories* (1942; Harmondsworth: Penguin Books, 1970), p. 146. Future references will appear in brackets in the text.

11. James W. Fernandez, 'Persuasions and Performances: Of the Beast in Everybody . . . And the Metaphors of Everyman', in Clifford Geertz (ed.), *Myth, Symbol and Culture* (New York: W. W. Norton & Co., 1971), p. 51.

12. Richard Poirier, *A World Elsewhere: The Place of Style in American Literature* (London: Chatto and Windus, 1967), p. 79.

13. Simone de Beauvoir, *The Second Sex*, (1949) trans. H. M. Parshley (New York: Bantam Books, 1961), p. 58.

14. Nina Baym, 'Melodramas of Beset Manhood: How Theories of American Literature Exclude Women Authors', in Elaine Showalter (ed.), *The New Feminist Criticism: Essays on Women, Literature and Theory* (London: Virago Press, 1986), pp. 63–80.

15. Ernest Hemingway, *The Old Man and the Sea* (1952; London, Triad Grafton Press, 1976), p. 23. Future references will appear in brackets in the text.

16. Judith Fetterley, *The Resisting Reader: A Feminist Approach to American Fiction* (Bloomington: Indiana University Press, 1978), p. xiii.

17. Annette Kolodny, ' "To Render Home a Paradise": Women on the New World Landscapes', in *Women's Language and Style*, ed. Douglas Butturff and Edmund L. Epstein (Akron, Ohio: L & S Books, 1978), p. 43.

18. Richard Clark, *History, Ideology and Myth in American Fiction, 1823–1852* (London: Macmillan, 1984), p. 10.

19. Clark, p. 12.

20. Tzvetan Todorov, *The Poetics of Prose*, (1971) trans. Richard Howard (Ithaca: Cornell University Press, 1977), p. 143.

21. Randall Jarrell, 'Children Selecting Books in a Library', *The Complete*

Poems (New York: Farrar, Strauss and Giroux, 1969), p. 107.
22. *The Art of the Novel*, p. 220.
23. Eleanor Hutchens, 'An Approach Through Time', in Mark Spilka (ed.), *Towards a Poetics of Fiction* (Bloomington and London: Indiana University Press, 1977), p. 61.
24. Quoted in Seymour Chatman, *Story and Discourse: Narrative Structure in Fiction and Film* (Ithaca and London: Cornell University Press, 1978), p. 53.
25. Gillespie, p. 120.
26. Auerbach, p. 214.
27. *Henry James: Letters*, IV, ed. Leon Edel (Cambridge, Mass. and London: Harvard University Press, 1984), 770.
28. Walter Benjamin, 'The Storyteller', *Illuminations*, (1955) trans. Henry Zohn, ed. Hannah Arendt (London: Fontana, 1973), p. 98.
29. Robert Scholes, 'An Approach Through Genre', in *Towards a Poetics of Fiction*, p. 48.
30. *The Art of the Novel*, p. 5.
31. James Early, *The Making of 'Go Down, Moses'* (Dallas: Southern Methodist University Press, 1972), p. 114, says that after the first printing of the book, 'And Other Stories' was dropped from the title, 'at Faulkner's request'. Early also says that 'Michael Millgate believes that the original title may have been an editor's rather than Faulkner's.'

7

Continuity and Change in the Southern Novella

by PETER MESSENT

1

In *Knight's Gambit*, Faulkner's title story in his 1949 collection, the florid outsider and bootlegger, Harriss, rebuilds an old plantation house six miles outside Jefferson, Mississippi, making it look like 'the Southern mansion in the moving pictures, only about five times as big and ten times as southern'.[1] Instead of raising corn and cotton, he raises pedigree stallions. Of his one-time father-in-law, to whom the land previously belonged, there remains only 'his home-made hickory rocking chair and the finger-prints on the calf bindings of books and the silver goblet he drank from'. These traces of the past are, in their turn, put aside: consigned as unwanted relics to—significantly—the attic.

In describing this mansion as 'a Before-the-War Hollywood set', Faulkner implies that—in Fredric Jameson's phrase— 'the historical referent' has been lost.[2] History has become the province of both nostalgia and pastiche. The mansion bears no relation to the actual history of the South, its lived experience, to 'the old fields' and 'one storey' galleried house. Instead, a false image of Southern life has been created, one that looks to Hollywood as its model. This is merely a 'pop image', a specious imitation, again to quote Jameson, 'of that history, which itself remains forever out of reach'.

Harriss may have 'destroyed' history, but Faulkner himself in *Knight's Gambit* does not. He keeps alive an awareness of the meaning of the past by his own authorial rôle and by his uses of the two principal figures of the novella, Gavin Stevens and his nephew Charles Mallison. Both uncle and nephew bear witness to an earlier way of life and community. They both share the memories and traditions of the Southern town, and are morally informed by that earlier way of life which Harriss physically obliterates. Their sense of Yoknapatawpha-Mississippi as their lineage contrasts vividly with the 'false' Southern past of Harriss's rebuilt mansion.

However, Stevens and Charles never *come to terms with* their Southern past in the comprehensive way that Ike McCaslin does in Faulkner's great novella, 'The Bear' (1942). This earlier novella, throughout, takes on much larger socio-historical issues: the relationship between the wilderness world and the social world which replaces it; slavery and its effect on Southern culture. In 'The Bear', Ike confronts these issues and transcends his past, emerges 'into historical self-consciousness'[3] as a result of that confrontation. In *Knight's Gambit* something far less momentous occurs. For Charles remains caught within the repetitions of history, his heroic aspirations in the Second World War depicted by the novella as merely naïve. His uncle's marriage does suggest a transcendence of the past, an ability to learn from his personal history to recover from previous mistakes, which lightly echoes Ike's. But his action occurs in a socio-historical vacuum, his age counters any real suggestion of hope for the future. Faulkner's literary model here, is uncomfortably close to the 'slick magazine serial' directly acknowledged in the text, with its 'stock characters', even its 'foreign fortune-hunter', and that version of the family romance which Faulkner charts here never strays far from the purely melodramatic. The resonances of Faulkner's earlier works are absent; Stevens's lesson learnt has more to do with compromise (accepting the intellectual limitations of his marital partner) than with transcendence; his action (marriage) a private and personal act, with no larger cultural implications.

The argument I wish to explore with regard to the Southern novella as a whole is that its thematic development parallels— and, because of the particular form of the novella, highlights—

that to be found in other forms of Southern fiction. An intermediary form, between the novel and the short story, the genre is marked by a 'combination of intensity and expansion'[4] resulting in a type of fiction which both focuses on a specific incident, or on an individual consciousness at a moment (or moments) of crisis, and from there circles outwards to reveal and examine the cultural conditions which give such an incident or crisis its larger meaning.

The thematic development to be found in the Southern novella is suggested in the comparison already made between the two Faulkner texts. There, one finds a movement in *Knight's Gambit* away from that strong concern with history and tradition that so marks 'The Bear' and the other major writing of the Southern Renaissance. This is replaced by a concern with the purely domestic (Stevens's marriage) which lacks larger cultural resonance. It is also replaced by an awareness of the possibility (with Harriss, the New Southerner) of a complete cutting of moorings between past and present. In *Knight's Gambit*, Faulkner's previous use of what Richard King defines as the Southern Family Romance (that 'collective fantasy' which made up the 'structure of feeling' of Southern culture)[5] is here completely dislocated by: the absence of a strong paternal figure; the concern with a complete confusion of family rôles marked by Faulkner early in the novella and evident in his presentation of the Harriss family and their affairs; the cultural alienation of all members of the Harriss family bar possibly the cipher-like mother; Charles's departure at the narrative's close. Stevens's marriage provides a positive resolution to the text in personal terms only.

Though this movement from the historical to the personal signals a decline in Faulkner's own writing, the same is not necessarily true of other Southern writers. Indeed, the very movement away from themes of history and tradition which occurs in Southern writing from the early 1940s onwards, can be seen in two ways. First, in terms of Harold Bloom's argument about 'the anxiety of influence', recent Southern writing may be engaged in a 'desire to escape the looming presence of precursors',[6] especially that of Faulkner himself. An escape from the influence of major literary ancestors is thus to be marked by a movement away from that concern with memory and history which is obsessively traced in Faulkner's writings, and—in less specific terms—by a literary desire to avoid the voice, theme, forms, associated with major Renaissance fiction generally.

Secondly, more recent Southern fiction may be read in broadly mimetic terms. Such a reading would stress the historical shift which has occurred in Southern society and culture since the Second World War. Louis D. Rubin, Jr. claims that—with its 'momentous social, political and economic' changes—the modern-day South 'in numerous respects seemed to bear little relationship to the community in which the leading writers of the Southern Renaissance had been born a half-century or so earlier'.[7] In this context, traditional Southern literary concerns with memory, tradition and history seemed increasingly irrelevant. As Donald R. Noble expresses it:

> There is more non-teleological thinking, less sense of a master plan. . . . concerns will move from communal to personal; and chaos and disorder that have been depicted in much Southern literature . . . as a rending of the social fabric . . . will now be seen in personal and domestic terms, not communal ones.[8]

This notion of the personal and domestic being more central than the communal is prefigured in *Knight's Gambit*; is prefigured, too, in James Agee's distinguished novella *The Morning Watch* (1951).

The concern for history found in the Southern Renaissance writing of the 1930s and 1940s has, then, been eroded in the modern Southern novella. If the Southern Family Romance provided earlier writers with a focus for their meditations on the past and its relation to the present, it can be seen that by 1955 (the end, approximately, of the main phase of the Southern Renaissance) the concern which pitted 'son against father, and often joined grandson and grandfather',[9] the concern with powerfully heroic father-figures at the centre of this Romance, has been greatly modified. Moreover, the historical consciousness that accompanies or runs alongside this concern, the patterns of recollection and repetition that mark so much of this Southern writing, are likewise much transformed.

2

Two brief illustrations of the historical concerns of Renaissance literature against which this changing focus in Southern writing can be located, are Andrew Lytle's novella *Alchemy* (1958) and, again, Faulkner's 'The Bear'. The former is a prime late example of that literary tradition which uncritically laments and mourns a wholeness imagined in the Southern past, though Lytle imaginatively translates his concern with Southern history to a much earlier South American colonial location. The materialism and self-willed determination that Lytle opposes to more traditional values bears clear relation to the author's own view of Southern history. Materialism, in the novella, triumphs with the defeat of Atahualpa by Pizzarro and De Soto's forces:

> That day a kind of alchemy was done. So it seems to me . . . whatever it was which on that day of triumph filled the eyes of those two captains, it seemed to them a thing of radiance, in white robes and most beautiful. But beside them there was in attendance a companion clad in a very different guise. As they reached out their hands to clasp their desires, that other—the dark thing—stepped forward to receive them.[10]

Those who impose their will on history and impose with that will the very character of modernity, bring alongside, and in symbiotic relationship with that modernity, spiritual and moral desolation: 'no longer would the stars be confused by the fires' glow. They were out—forever out'.

In contrast to this novella, though also centrally concerned with both history and tradition, is Faulkner's 'The Bear' (1942). Ike McCaslin frees himself from the past's burdens by directly confronting that past. In Richard King's words:

> Ike literally 'remembers' a past which belongs to him and his family. Once acknowledged and worked through ('He knew what he was going to find before he found it'), his past is transcended and becomes 'other'. He is free of it.

Ike replaces his own grandfather (and the crimes of incest and miscegenation with which he is—as dominant 'will' in the family—associated) by a new 'spiritual' authority, Sam Fathers. Faulkner uses the Family Romance to explore in an analytical manner Ike's Southern historical and racial heritage, an exploration which leads in the direction not of mourning the past, but of understanding and transcending it.

3

The movement away from this strong concern with history and the father-son relationship which so often accompanies it is signalled not only by Faulkner himself in *Knight's Gambit*, but also by Robert Penn Warren in *The Circus in the Attic* (1952), whose central protagonist, Bolton Loveheart, ends up like the father-in-law's belongings in Faulkner's novella, 'at home' only in the attic of his family house, cut adrift from contemporary history (the Hiroshima bombing 'meant nothing'[11] to him), in a world of personal and private meaning with no bridge available to the social world. His knowledge of local history is of no help in his failure to cope with the demands of everyday life. He finds contentment alone in an upstairs room with his memories—personal and historical—of a world in which he has never for long been able to fit, with painted representations (his symbolic circus) of that fullness of life which he has never been able fully to share.

The Circus in the Attic focuses on those themes of loneliness and isolation which will come to replace—but which in this text run alongside—themes of memory and history. Bolton Loveheart is aware as local historian of a familial and historical context to which he belongs, but he is unable to make the connections which would render his life meaningful in the present. The questions he wishes to ask his father, a member of the civil war generation (*'Father, did it hurt when you were shot . . . Father, did you ever talk to General Forrest—'*), only leap to mind when his father is dying, when they can no longer be asked. Family, community, nature, religion, do not sustain Loveheart in any way. Although there is a slightly uneasy tone to this novella (particularly revealed in the narrative's closure)—suggesting perhaps Penn Warren's unwillingness to accept all the implications of his text—what the fiction most fully reveals is a sense of 'debilitating alienation'[12] brought about by the complete breaking down of older beliefs, forms and relationships.

The uncomfortable yoking in Penn Warren's novella of a central theme of displacement and estrangement with an implicit desire for coherent continuity in history gives way in post-Renaissance writing to a greater preoccupation with themes of alienation. Place, family and past still, as Martha E. Cook claims, appear more significant thematically in Southern fiction from 1950 to 1981 than in other regional writing, and as she also points out: 'Southern fiction may not be as distinctive as it was during the Renaissance, yet one does not confuse writers of this generation with John Updike or Norman Mailer.'[13]

But, as the South has changed, so the concerns of Southern fiction have changed. New voices have appeared, voices trying to locate themselves not just in the context of local memory and history (the traditional Southern themes), but also—sometimes exclusively—'trying to find their place in an apparently meaningless and absurd universe'.[14] While in William Styron's longer fiction, for example, a distinctively Southern voice appears and regional difference remains central subject, complementing and contrasting with his existentialist themes, in his novella *The Long March* (1952) Styron's voice could almost be mistaken for Norman Mailer's, with particular reference to *The Naked and the Dead* (1948).

This apparent anomaly can be directly explained by Styron's use of the novella form. That 'effect of singleness and intensity',[15] which belongs to the novella form, attaches itself in *The Long March* to the specific narrative purpose of that text: an allegorical examination of the conflict between the institutional and the individual. Templeton's 'absolute and unquestioned authority' is set against Mannix, who rebels against this authority which he regards as being exercised for absurd ends and associated with a careless disregard for human life. This carelessness is signalled at the narrative's start with eight deaths, boys reduced to 'shreds of bone, gut, and dangling tissue' as a result of 'some short rounds' being dropped 'on a chow-line' during a training exercise 'in the States in peace-time',[16] the early 1950s. Mannix's rebellion on behalf of the individual spirit, though potentially and in effect just as 'absurd' as that authority exercised, is condoned by the narrator, Culver. He apostrophizes 'Old Al' at the narrative's end as 'the man with the back unbreakable, the soul of pity' even though he clearly realizes the futility of Mannix's rebellion, asking 'where was he now, great unshatterable vessel of longing, lost in the night, astray at mid-century in the never-endingness of war?'

The Southern setting—the Carolina marine base—is of minimal importance here; it is, as Sheldon Sacks calls it, 'the apologue'[17] that is central. In almost every respect *The Long March* is a perfect illustration of the novella form. The limited focus of the text, its intense examination of an absurd world and the conditions of absurdity as represented by the Mannix-Templeton conflict lead to an illumination of a single subject whose implications are then examined in depth. The movement between the expansive (the existential universe) and the intensive (the immediate conflict) which so marks the genre is clearly marked here, and social background (beyond the immediate army context) almost entirely disappears.

In Truman Capote's *Breakfast at Tiffany's* (1958) we enter alien fictional territory, other rooms; not Gavin Stevens's 'lawyer's office', nor Loveheart's attic, both of which bear closer or lesser relationship to the Southern community which surrounds, and in the former sustains, them, but rooms in 'a brownstone in the East Seventies'[18] in New York. Estrangement here is suggested by setting. Holly Golightly is in Capote's symbolic scheme, a bird who cannot be caged ('If you let yourself love a wild thing,' she tells Joe Bell, 'You'll end up looking at the sky'). 'Home', she tells the narrator, 'is where you feel at home. I'm still looking.' Married at 14 to a husband old enough to be her father, she soon takes off from Tulip, West Texas, to Hollywood, from there to New York, and from there to Brazil. The novella opens with the narrator being shown a photograph of an African wood sculpture of a girl's head 'the spit-image of Holly Golightly' taken some ten years after her departure from New York, and suggesting both her continued exoticism and her continued instability, lack of meaningful context to her life. William Nance describes Holly's values as 'those of the Capote-narrator: she is a part of himself set free like a broken-stringed kite to wander towards an ambiguous land of dreams and death'.[19]

The Southern connections in this novella (those both of Holly and of the narrator, a young writer implicitly Southern, who has 'so recently escaped the regimentation of a small town') are seen primarily as restrictive, and Holly is defined against a New

York landscape composed of various grotesques: the 'absurd foetus' Rutherford Trawler; the stuttering six-footer from Wildwood, Arkansaw, Mag; the formal and exotic Brazilian with presidential aspirations, José Ybarra-Jaeger. Capote's world is one in which death ('the fat woman') and exotic romance, sexuality and innocent naïveté, go hand in hand; a world where all sense of memory and history is translated to the personal realm only (Holly's memory of her brother, the narrator's of Holly). Disconnection, homelessness, alienation, are dominant motifs here: Holly's room, with its 'fly-by-night look', suitcases and unpacked crates its only furniture, suggests the impermanence which is so central to Holly's depiction. Capote illustrates that recent Southern fiction which has moved away from regional concerns to confront more general issues of identity and meaning in a modern American landscape where notions of tradition, ritual and community need both re-examination and re-definition.

4

Such re-examinations occur, this time in a more distinctly Southern setting, in Barry Hannah's exciting recent novella *Ray* (1980). Here, Hannah's postmodernist concerns lead to a disruption of the traditional novella form. If the question of 'voice' is all important in Southern fiction—and I will return soon to this issue—then Hannah's novella presents 'a fragmented vision, told by a "voice" that seems to have lost all faith in order'.[20] This voice, that of the main protagonist, Ray, is difficult in itself to pin down:

> Ray, you are a doctor and you are in a hospital in Mobile, except now you are a patient but you're still me. Say what? You say you want to know who I am?[21]

It is also a voice which moves wildly within time, from Civil War to Vietnam: 'Oh, help me!', it requests at one point, 'I am losing myself in two centuries and two wars.' Though the voice and its concerns are distinctively Southern, neither identity nor the relation of voice to memory and to historical context ('I roam in the past for my best mind') can be coherently defined here. One individual is described purely in terms of his humming:

Maybe there are worse guys than me, he [De Soto] said to himself. For example the guy from Minnesota who hummed all the time. He seemed to be furnishing the score for every puny adventure of his life. Always the hum. . . There was a tune for feeding his cat, another for his goldfish, another for watering the plants in his crummy color-clashing apartment. He had no radio or phonograph. His time with women was limited—by them. But on he hummed incessantly, arrogantly, until somebody broke his mouth at a graveside ceremony one afternoon.

The hum makes for consistency, but certainly not for identity. However, the tone of the passage suggests the comic tone of the novella as a whole, which strays, with surrealistic wit ('She won a Sony T.V. by coming in third on a mass-murderer quiz in *Oui* magazine') through fragmentary glimpses at Ray's fragmentary life (lives). Hannah—in presenting Ray, doctor, patient, alcoholic, Vietnam veteran, womanizer, vigilante, jet-stealer, father—juxtaposes linguistic and narrative units in highly original and unexpected ways, ways which deny normal readerly expectation of coherence and orderliness.

Born in Jackson, Mississippi, and living in Tuscaloosa, Ray both shares the prejudices of his region ('visiting Lee's Tomb a lot and taking in too much sound and bourbon') and of his nation. Watching Westy's son (quarterback for Murrah High in Jackson) play football, the first time Ray has seen a high-school game since playing himself, he remembers getting knocked 'over a fence and on to a cinder track . . . by some hulking freak who later found his way to the Chicago Bears'. He continues: 'That was my last punt return, and I went seriously into Fine Art after that, where you could play with yourself and get applauded for it.' The novella gives glimpses of Ray's rôle as American Civilization teacher, civil war combatant ('I live', he tells us, 'in so many centuries. Everybody is still alive'), poet, sexual adventurer, and foot fetishist.

The novella is postmodernist in both form and content. There is no centre here, either in terms of Ray's own 'identity' ('Hold old Ray close, everybody, for he is estranged from the clear home that he once knew'), or in terms of the traditional novella, which according to both J. H. E. Paine and Judith Leibowitz operates around a 'turning point, when the work begins to turn back on itself in redevelopment'.[22] Hannah, here, reworks the novella form, intensity giving way to fragmentation, to fit concerns which can be read as 'postmodernist'. Such a re-working points to the difficulties of actually defining, despite the efforts of Paine and others, the novella. Robert Boyers in his *Atrocity and Amnesia: The Political Novel Since 1945* (1985) speaks of the difficulty of 'uncovering the laws and precise limits' of the novel as a genre, and what he says can be applied to the novella, too. 'The very form of the novel', he says, 'is routinely called into question by its most ambitious practitioners in a degree unmatched in the other literary arts'.[23] Here, Hannah embarks on a similar re-formulation of the novella, expanding and questioning the traditional limits of the genre.

Fredric Jameson defines postmodernism as a cultural movement in which 'the alienation of the subject is displaced by the fragmentation of the subject', a concern realized in this text by the uncertainty and lack of unity of Ray's 'voice'. Jameson also discusses the importance of pastiche in such writing. The historical concern found in Southern Renaissance literature— and in Faulkner's 'The Bear' in particular—is, in Jameson's terms, an acknowledgement and examination of 'the retrospective dimension indispensible to any vital reorientation of our collective future'. This concern is replaced (and he is referring here to E. L. Doctorow's *Ragtime*, in particular), by a reading imposed by a novel which makes it:

> virtually impossible for us to reach and to thematize those official 'subjects' which float above the text but cannot be integrated into our reading of the sentences. In that sense, not only does the novel resist interpretation, it is organized systematically and formally to short-circuit an older type of social and historical interpretation which it perpetually holds out and withdraws.

Ray is a very different kind of text than *Ragtime* but the comments above are helpful, I think, in approaching it. The 'official' subject of the novella is the relationship—in historical terms—between Southern individual (Ray) and the patterns of contemporary Southern culture; between Ray and Southern and national history—the founding of Tuscaloosa, the Civil War, Vietnam. This relationship is both held out to the reader and short-circuited by the very organization, the cutting of moorings effected both by the creation of a text which operates in the manner of surrealistic collage, and by the use of a voice which is unsure of its own location. The novella is finally, despite such insecurities, both optimistic and exhilarating as Ray doggedly perseveres with his twentieth-century Alabama existence. But the last line of the novella, 'Sabers, gentlemen, sabers', in effect only reveals how little connection holds floating present to floating past. Hannah, while writing in a clearly Southern context, denies the worth or validity of that historical referent so vital to an earlier generation of writers.

5

Ray's voice, in Hannah's novella, is explicitly misogynistic at times ('Women enjoy revenge more than the worst Apache', 'Women are fucking awful'), and it is noticeable that in the majority of the novellas so far discussed, all written from within a white Southern male tradition, women are either treated disparagingly or absent from the text's centre. Capote is the one exception.

'To have a voice is to have a self', Anne Goodwyn Jones asserts in *Tomorrow is Another Day: The Woman Writer in the South, 1859–1936* (1981),[24] and it is clear that there are other voices to be heard, other identities to be defined, apart from those already discussed, in the Southern literary tradition. The novella form is one that has apparently remained generally unpractised by Southern black writers, the literary voices of one group long denied their place in Southern history (if we define history, with Anne Jones, as having 'a rôle in the public world'[25]). The genre, though, has been used by women writing in the South—Katherine Anne Porter, Eudora Welty and Carson McCullers—and I would like to consider whether, as Jones suggests in the context of the writers she examines in her book, such fiction can be seen as 'a strategy for speaking truths publicly'[26] on the part of those denied the normal channels of public utterance, on behalf of their disinherited group.

Indeed, it becomes clear that when—as in Porter's case—a Southern woman writer uses the novella form in order to provide a critique of the dominant Southern culture, such a critique emerges—as one might expect—not through any explicit thematic concern with political or public life, but out of a concern for gender rôles, often presented in a *domestic* context (which then leads outwards in the direction of larger cultural analysis). What is perhaps surprising here is the very partial applicability of Anne Jones's model.[27] Though each of the three writers I now want to examine is centrally concerned with the issue of gender rôle, only Katherine Anne Porter pursues this interest in the direction of thorough-going analysis of woman's rôle within a patriarchal culture. Eudora Welty's *The Ponder Heart*—though open to ironic reading—is, on the face ot it, uncritical of Southern society and its institutions, while Carson McCullers's novellas are so focused around notions of personal *abnormality* that they remain finally resistant to readings concerned with the notion of *cultural* norms, their strengths and weaknesses. In this respect, McCullers shows herself precocious in her literary concerns, in her very early abandonment of the 'traditional' Southern themes of memory and history.

In *'Gone with the Wind* and Others: Popular Fiction, 1920 to 1950', Anne Jones remarks that

> In general, the men take history, and the women gender, as the means for their meditations on past and present.... Men assumed a rôle in the public world, hence in history; women assumed a private rôle, profoundly shaped by gender and (until recently) outside history.

This statement might start to suggest why the novella form has particularly suited the artistic needs of some Southern women writers. For—whether or not using the form to provide a critique of Southern culture—the position of women 'outside history' has led to a specific concern in much of their fiction with the domestic environment: home and family used as the context in which issues of power and authority, of traditional gender and familial rôles and their limitations can be explored. It is in this context that the 'conventions that prescribe specifically southern womanhood' (Anne Jones) can be set against the needs and urges of the individual self. And—in Porter's fiction certainly—one can go on to show how an exploration of those 'domestic' limits (a term used in no derogatory way here) can lead directly to a critique of Southern cultural institutions, and in particular of the patriarchy and the sexual and social oppression associated with it.

The confined limits (in terms of the opposition between public and private, history and gender) within which much of Southern women's fiction works, the domestic context it so often uses as location, suggests why the boundaries of the novella form so suit it. Though authors such as Faulkner, Conrad and Mann do use what Paine calls 'the "generally distinct effect" of intensity and expansion' to move between a constant focus on a specific subject and a concern with explicitly economic and historical issues of a 'public' nature, such types of expansiveness are unusual, such concerns being more commonly the province of the novel (it is noticeable that excepting 'The Bear', the novellas I have examined and which I see as representative, have avoided the issue of black-white relationships, *the* major theme of Southern history).[28] The limited boundaries of the novella form have best suited those examinations of an individual consciousness or a particular thematic issue (often, in the more traditional Southern version, concerning the effect of past on present), conducted within a tightly controlled environment. If a concern with gender in the Southern woman's novella (as a point of entry for Porter and Welty into cultural analysis, for McCullers as a reference point for themes of emotional dislocation and personal alienation) is allied with the limited, and often domestic, context in which that examination occurs, then it is clear why the novella should be so successfully utilized by these writers, becoming, for Porter and McCullers, at least, their most successfully practised literary form.

A series of limited environments contain Miranda in Porter's *Old Mortality* (1940). The convent in which (borrowing a word from the anti-Catholic propaganda that has fallen into her hands) she sees herself as 'immured'[29] is one of a series of confining locations—the home, the hotel room, the railway carriage—and 'hideous institution[s]', as Cousin Eva describes the family, which hem Miranda in on all sides. Miranda, a central character whose isolation becomes more and more explicit in the text, joins that series of isolated protagonists to be found in so much Southern women's fiction. Her growing sense of self, her move towards maturity and understanding (strongly qualified here, it must be said, by an ironic narrative voice which holds the protagonist at clear distance, yet which—in

presenting the conditions of Miranda's rebellion—confirms the
need for such redefinitions of self), carries with it a strong
attack on a society rigidly organized in terms of gender rôles
and expectations. Though Miranda may still be both arrogant
and ignorant at the novella's closure, her need to escape a
Southern family which is seen as both constricting in the rôles
and opportunities given its female members and stagnating in
the sense of its over-concern with the past, with family history,
is the central subject matter of the text. And the strength of
feeling and desperation which concludes in her final declaration
to herself, 'I can't live in their world [the world of the family
past and, by extension, the limitations of that world] any
longer',[30] strongly counters the ironic context in which that
declaration is placed through the use of that more knowing
voice which controls and encloses the narrative.

This novella, like so many texts of the Southern Renaissance,
centrally concerns itself with *memory*, with the effect of past on
present. And the models of Southern womanhood and of family
structure which Miranda has available (in this novella which
focuses on memories of the *family*) lead her to cast off her past
and deny her memories at the conclusion of the narrative. 'Her
most inner and secret mind' rejects the lessons of her father and
her Cousin Eva. She judges them as

> aliens who lectured her and admonished her, who loved her with
> bitterness and denied her the right to look at the world with her
> own eyes, who demanded that she accept their version of life and
> yet could not tell her the truth, not in the smallest thing,

and says to herself, in a climactic final moment of the novella,
'*I will be free of them, I shall not even remember them.*' Freedom is
here seen by Miranda as the ability to put memory entirely
behind her, a questionable virtue in terms of what Richard
King calls, in his discussion of Faulkner's 'The Bear', 'the
psychoanalytic task of transforming repetitions into recollection'.
Miranda's final immaturity is suggested in her use of the word
'aliens': she cannot interpret or fully gain access to the past, her
rejection of it is hasty and ill-informed. She casts herself loose of
her family, her marriage, her cultural inheritance, but with no
comprehensive understanding of the failures of that inheritance
on which to build for the future. Memory is essential for an

emergence into full self-consciousness. In denying memory, Miranda loses all purchase upon the past and moves, autonomous but bereft of moral or cultural locating points, into the future. The ironic frame of the novella thus carries strong suggestions that Miranda's 'freedom' is a heavily mixed blessing.

This perhaps projects the reader forward into some of Porter's other novellas, *Noon Wine*, *Pale Horse, Pale Rider*, *The Leaning Tower*, and *The Cracked Looking Glass*, where, to generalize, a past tradition is now recognized as completely unavailable to the main protagonists, crumbling at his or her touch like that leaning tower given central symbolic status in the novella of that name.[31] No sense of a full or coherent cultural tradition is to be found in these texts and the heavy presence of death which dominates this fiction—death seen in *Pale Horse, Pale Rider* in potentially comforting terms—suggests, I speculate, a deep dissatisfaction on Porter's part with a world in which the traditional certainties have disappeared.

The double-bind, of course, is that she shows through her use of Miranda as central protagonist in *Old Mortality*, the failings— in a Southern context at least—of this traditional world. For the novella clearly shows the restrictive boundaries of traditional Southern society and their inadequacies for any woman of intelligence and imagination. Anne Jones points in *Tomorrow is Another Day* to the 'persistent dialectic' between realism and romanticism in Southern woman's fiction before 1936, and such a dialectic is encoded in *Old Mortality* in the opposition between Aunt Amy and Cousin Eva: Amy, now dead, 'only a ghost in a [photograph] frame, and a sad, pretty story from the old times'; Eva never 'a belle', but still (in the third part of the novella) alive and kicking, now a thin and crotchety 'old maid'. Amy, whose story Miranda begins to piece together from the 'floating ends of narrative' she hears, is a romantic figure. Her early death and long courtship with Uncle Gabriel make her, to Miranda and her sister Maria, someone belonging 'to the world of poetry'. She is the epitome of the Southern belle: a beauty according to the type the girls have been brought up to admire:

> A beauty must be a good dancer, superb on horseback, with a serene manner, an amiable gaiety. . . . Beautiful teeth and hands, of course, and over and above all this some mysterious crown of enchantment that attracted and held the heart.

'The function of southern womanhood', historians agree, 'has been to justify the perpetuation of the hegemony of the male sex, the upper and middle classes, and the white race'. Amy's function in her society is clearly ornamental, her supposed rôle to offer her softly submissive self to a 'strong, commanding, intelligent and dominant man'[32] in this strongly patriarchal society. Even Miranda and Maria find themselves from childhood judged according to ornamental function first and foremost ('Father . . . pushed them away if they had not freshly combed hair and nicely scrubbed finger-nails. "Go away, you're disgusting," he would say . . .').

Amy is clearly aware of the narrowness of her rôle. Ironically stating that 'what I need is a good dancing partner to guide me through life', she consciously responds to Gabriel's praise of her physical appearance—'I love your hair, Amy, the most beautiful hair in the world'—by immediately cropping it close to her head. She cannot, however, escape this rôle, her mother assuring her in the light of her dissatisfaction 'that marriage and children would cure her of everything', her only presented alternative being that of old maid. Her marriage, however, is followed swiftly by her death, a death which Eva much later suggests may have been a suicide undertaken in the light of 'some disgrace, some exposure that she faced'. If she is sexually promiscuous—and it is clear that we are to be left *between* versions of Amy's life, never finally to know 'what was the end of this story?'—again the implication is that it is in rebellion against the confining rôles open to her in a society which prescribed womanhood in such narrow terms, and which operated according to an 'evasive idealism that pushes reality aside'. Once Amy is dead, the possible scandal behind her death buried with her body, she can, and does, become, to all but Eva, a figure of complete romance. Her beauty—a beauty always seen in Southern culture as 'irrelevant to the serious business of life'[33]—is what posthumously defines her: 'a singing angel', 'the griefs of old mortality' left behind her.

Cousin Eva, in comparison, is—in the eyes of Maria and Miranda when young girls—'a blot' who belongs to 'their everyday world of dull lessons to be learned', the world of realism. Physically graceless, no rôle save that of old maid is available for her culturally, and she is seen—by both males and females in the family—to take to the cause of female suffrage in compensation for her lack of value in terms of ornamentation. Her view of the parties and dances of her girlhood as a marriage 'market' again strikes an anti-romantic chord. She remembers girls as being obsessed by their sexual attractiveness only, abusing their own bodies because of the cultural demands of physical perfection: Amy

> drinking lemon and salt to stop her periods when she wanted to go to dances. There was a superstition among young girls about that. They fancied that young men could tell what ailed them by touching their hands.

Eva is not, however, to Miranda's mind, an attractive figure. Her attitude is affected, so Miranda sees, by anger and perhaps jealousy; her 'strong character' is judged 'deforming'. She has succeeded within limits in the political world by her courage and persistence, but at the cost of a certain isolation from her larger society—'it almost made a pariah of me', she admits. Her career is not presented, by Miranda at least, as offering an alternative rôle to that of Amy's, and Miranda finds herself finally with 'no place' in this family—either in the traditional rôles offered her by her culture and against which Amy has defined herself or in the political rôle offered her by her cousin.

What is very noticeable about this novella, is its chronological setting (1885–1912), Amy's death occurring in memory, prior to the actual start of the narrative. Porter is looking to an older South to examine its failings in terms of gender rôles offered. And that examination of rôles does point in the direction of a stern critique of sexual oppression in a patriarchal tradition, of a clear realization of the failings of the conventions which prescribe Southern womanhood to allow for the needs of any more than partial expression of the individual self.

With this text, Porter herself appears to leave behind the Southern past as central material for her novellas, as if, with Miranda, no model for the construction of new female rôle and identity is to be found in that fictional territory. And, although Southern cultural institutions are seriously questioned in this text, the notion of any proposal of a liberal ideology which Anne Jones suggests can accompany such questionings appears particularly muted. The intensity of the concentration on the figure

of Miranda herself and the family structure which surrounds
her (ideal territory for the novella form) does not lead her in the
direction of either racial or political themes (Eva is finally a
marginalized figure) and the cultural critique which is apparent
leads, as I have suggested, not in the direction of cultural
transformation, but in that of individual alienation.

The delight in the provincial and in the rituals of the small
community (the trial), the comic affection for her Southern
materials, which mark Eudora Welty's *The Ponder Heart* (1953),
suggests that the satiric effect present in this novella is not
offered in the same spirit of that serious cultural critique found
in Porter. The subtle social gradations in this small-town
Mississippi community are clearly marked, with Edna Earle
saying, for example, of lawyer Gladney: 'He says to me, "Mizriz
Ponder?" That's what he calls me Mizriz. He likes to act
country, but he don't have all that far to go—he *is* country.'[34]
But these differences are always presented in the spirit of
comedy, and despite her accusation of others as 'small-town',
Edna Earle's is presented as very much of a parochial voice,
and the humour constantly operates on a similar level. Miss
Teacake Magee's evidence, for example, at Daniel Ponder's
trial for the murder of his wife (who, it emerges, he has acci-
dently tickled—playing 'creep-mousie'—to death), is interrupted by the judge asking for a show of hands for dinner ('I
made a little sign to Ada's sister', Edna adds, 'she'd better kill a
few more hens').

Despite Daniel's overgenerous nature and the fact that he is
simple-minded to the point of possible insanity, there is no
questioning of gender rôles here, or, indeed, of any need for
societal change: indeed, the changes that do occur are un-
welcome. Daniel's 'fond and loving [Ponder] heart' is the centre
of spontaneous vitality in the story where Edna, 'go-between
between . . . family and the world', is the one who helps manage
his life and deal with his mistakes, acts as what Peggy Whitman
Prenshaw calls, in relation to the rôle of women in Welty's
fiction as a whole, the agent of 'memory and tradition'[35] in a
gender relationship equally satisfactory to both parties. And,
despite the ironic twist at the conclusion of the narrative, Uncle
Daniel isolated because of his very generosity, this comic monologue is one very much written in a spirit of affection rather

than criticism, exposing, with 'genial humanity . . . the small vanities, follies, blunders, incongruities' of southern small-town life. The very nature of the comic monologue leads away from the sophistication and flexibility of style which mark Eudora Welty's other fictions, but the intensity of her concentration on the parochial here is perhaps in line with what Ruth M. Vande Kieft holds to be 'the curious lack of a social or political attitude'[36] in her work as a whole.

In Carson McCullers's novellas *Reflections in a Golden Eye* (1940) and *The Ballad of the Sad Café* (1943) the subject of gender relations is again central. And again, it is through McCullers's use of the microcosmic (the relations between six people on a southern army post in peacetime in the former novella; the café and the relations between Amelia, Lymon, Marvin, and surrounding community in the latter) that this subject is pursued. The intensity of effect thus conveyed—with this use of closed communities and limited relationships—clearly marks out McCullers's use of the novella form. Her explorations of gender rôles and community mores in these contexts lead though in the direction of dead ends: to violence, alienation and isolation. Her concern with gender rôles in traditional communities extends in the direction of that concern with debilitating alienation which Porter suggests, a concern which has become central to Southern fiction in recent years. Small Southern community plays a primary rôle, though, in *Old Mortality*; in McCullers it plays a *secondary* rôle to the 'grotesque' characters and behaviour which are of central interest to her. She does question in her fiction the traditional rigidities of Southern social and sexual hierarchies; the new life and energy which are allowed to surface and replace such rigidities are, however, brief lived, and in *The Ballad of the Sad Café* what is left behind is a rural culture in terminal decline. But it is the concern with loss and loneliness which is her most central subject, with individuals who *finally* are in no way defined by their cultural context. And gender relations in McCullers reinforce her message of *personal* dislocation and loss of centre as the very conditions of twentieth-century life, a dislocation realized in 'parable'[37] form by her use of protagonists who are disfigured either physically, psychologically, or both.

In *The Ballad of the Sad Café*, then, the café, run by Amelia—

with the hunchback dwarf Lymon as its live centre—becomes the town's centre of vitality. Here, the cheapness and misery of small-town rural life, the 'one dim scramble just to get the things needed to keep alive',[38] is countered by this utopian and 'precious' locale, where pleasure and delight are the rule rather than the exception:

> the café was the warm centre point of the town. . . . Almost everyone came to the café at least once during the week. . . . There . . . the deep bitter knowing that you are not worth much in this world could be laid low.

This rejuvenation of a community, a recentring of the community on a different unit (based on 'fellowship, the satisfactions of the belly, and a certain gaiety and grace of behaviour') than that of the traditional family, in a location where normal gender and social hierarchies become irrelevant, is dependent for its continued existence on the relationship between Amelia and Lymon.

Love is at the centre of McCullers's fictional world and it is always one-sided. Amelia's possession of many masculine characteristics has condemned her—until Lymon's arrival—to a life of emotional disconnection. The story of her marriage to Marvin is one of sexual misunderstanding. Far from toning down her temper and putting, as the town expects, 'a bit of bride-fat' on her, the experience merely confirms her masculine traits (she reads 'The Farmer's Almanac', smokes her father's pipe downstairs, and avoids sharing the marital bed with Marvin). The end of the relationship is signalled when:

> Towards evening [Marvin] came in drunk, went up to Miss Amelia with wet wide eyes, and put his hand on her shoulder. He was trying to tell her something, but before he could open his mouth she had swung once with her fist and hit his face so hard that he was thrown back against the wall and one of his front teeth was broken.

Amelia—businesswoman, carpenter, distiller—'dressed in overalls and gumboots' and standing six foot two inches tall, finds temporary happiness and love with Cousin Lymon. Her failure to fill an ornamental function but willingness to submit herself to his varying demands (carrying him on her back in the swamp, for example), leads to a relationship in which gender rôles are peculiarly distributed, but which forms the basis both for Amelia's greater happiness and sociability and for the burgeoning of the café and its importance to the local community.

McCullers's explorations of alternative gender rôles and forms of community vitality swiftly collapse, though, with Marvin's re-entry on to the scene, Lymon's fascination and Amelia's fight with him. Amelia consigns herself consequently to self-imposed imprisonment in the upstairs room of the now closed and collapsing café building. So, though McCullers shows her concern with issues of sexual and social position and authority here, and in *Reflections in a Golden Eye*, these are clearly subordinated to her stress on the individual heart. Her use of the 'grotesque' cuts strongly against any realistic reading of the texts, and means that no norm is offered the reader against which he or she can measure the excesses of the characters. Though the voice recounting the narrative of *The Ballad of the Sad Café* is one that appears to represent the community, the reader is curiously dislocated by a narrative which suggests that the Amelia-Lymon relationship brings new vitality to this community (the pairing becoming temporarily, at least, one which—through Amelia's love—positively transforms an entire township), yet which also suggests that this relationship is abnormal in terms of Amelia's aberrant sexuality.[39]

Love has a transforming power in this text, but no general statements are possible about McCullers's final attitudes towards gender rôles or towards the conditions of Southern culture because of the lack of normative models against which her grotesques can be measured. It is the difficulty of contact and communication which is her subject, together with the power of love as potential medium for transcending alienation. Her use of 'grotesques' is a way of suggesting both the level of difficulty of the former, the very force of the latter. Finally, though, her fictions close with death, derangement, isolation; alienation is seen as the end condition of individual existence in a Southern world where social and individual bondings are presented as merely superficial or temporary.

And in this sense, we see some similarities in the patternings of women's novellas in the South, and those of their male counterparts. Though the former define their fictional territory in the province of the domestic and centre their fictions on the

issue of gender rôles, while male writers show an explicit awareness of issues of political power and mastery at a public level
('The Bear', *Alchemy*), and a more overt concern (in *Ray* and *The
Circus in the Attic*) with notions of public history, nonetheless, a
common ground is shared by both. First, Katherine Anne
Porter, at least, in *Old Mortality* shares with her Southern
Renaissance male contemporaries a central concern with issues
of memory and the past, the problem of locating oneself against
the world of the parent (particularly the father) and the grand-
parent, although she then proceeds to turn away from the
regional specificity which continues to mark their work. Second,
in the more recent Southern novella and in those earlier writers
moving away from Renaissance concerns, notions of history and
tradition seem increasingly meaningless, or in McCullers's case,
irrelevant, and writers of both genders interest themselves, not
with the way an individual is centrally placed *in relation to* his or
her culture, but with a depiction of cultural context as a setting
against which issues of dislocation, loss of coherent identity and
fragmentation can be pursued. Barry Hannah trades in the
surreal and post-modern as a way of treating these concerns, so
retaining an ability to thematically examine the literal breakdown of cultural and historical context. McCullers, earlier,
roots her work in the grotesque, a technique which has the effect
of lending to her fiction an exceptionally claustrophobic air as
the personal is thus ultimately divorced from the larger political
or cultural arena.

In all the texts examined, however, despite divergencies of
thematic concern and despite the increasing cultural homogenization of the nation as a whole, a clear Southern voice can still
be heard. Fictional concerns and techniques have continued to
emerge which can certainly be located as regionally specific. As
Donald R. Noble says, 'for every sign of homogenization, there
is equal evidence that Southern life retains traditions and values,
attitudes and accents that will be a long time in the erasing.'
The Southern writer is still, as Martha E. Cook observes, more
concerned 'in significant thematic ways with place, family, and
past'[40] than other regional writers, and both a distinctively
Southern voice and humour still continue to demarcate the
Southern novella from other American examples of the genre.

NOTES

1. William Faulkner, *Knight's Gambit* (London: Chatto and Windus, 1969), p. 135.
2. Fredric Jameson, 'Postmodernism, or the Cultural Logic of Late Capitalism', in *New Left Review* (Vol. 146, 1984), 53–128.
3. Richard King, *A Southern Renaissance: The Cultural Awakening of the American South, 1930–1955* (New York, Oxford: Oxford University Press, 1980), p. 135.
4. J. H. E. Paine, *Theory and Criticism of the Novella* (Bonn: Bouvier Verlag Herbert Grundmann, 1979), p. 106.
5. *A Southern Renaissance*, p. 27. The term is fully explained here, pp. 26–38.
6. Richard King uses these phrases in his discussion of Harold Bloom in *A Southern Renaissance*, pp. 139–40. Though Dr. King is writing here of Faulkner and his contemporaries and their response to an historical past, his remarks may be modified to fit a generation of Southern writers who are, in turn, responding to Faulkner—their *literary* 'father'—and his influence.
7. Louis D. Rubin, Jnr., Blyden Jackson, Rayburn S. Moore, Lewis P. Simpson, Thomas Daniel Young (eds.), *The History of Southern Literature* (Baton Rouge and London: Louisiana State University Press, 1985), pp. 463–64.
8. Donald R. Noble, 'The Future of Southern Writing', in *The History of Southern Literature*, p. 587.
9. Richard King, *A Southern Renaissance*, p. 35. I depend heavily on Dr. King's excellent book at this point of my argument.
10. Andrew Lytle, *Alchemy*, in *A Novel, A Novella, and Four Stories* (New York: McDowell, Obolesky Inc., 1958), pp. 163–64. Lytle, it should be noted, was one of the original Nashville Agrarians.
11. Robert Penn Warren, *The Circus in the Attic and Other Stories* (London: Eyre and Spottiswoode, 1952), p. 60.
12. David Marion Holman uses this phrase in discussing Peter Taylor's fiction in *The History of Southern Literature*, p. 496.
13. Martha E. Cook, 'Old Ways and New Ways', in *The History of Southern Literature*, p. 534.
14. Thomas Daniel Young, 'A Second Generation of Novelists', ibid., p. 466.
15. Judith Leibowitz, *Narrative Purpose in the Novella*, quoted in Paine, *Theory and Criticism of the Novella*, p. 120.
16. William Styron, *The Long March* (London: Corgi Books, 1980), pp. 7, 15, 9.
17. Mary Doyle Springer explicates Sacks's term in *Form of the Modern Novella* ' "Apologue" makes use of the characters and what happens to them to maximize "the truth of a statement or statements", a principle which other critics variously call "allegory", "parable", or sometimes "fable" '. Quoted in Paine, *Theory and Criticism of the Novella*, p. 67.
18. Truman Capote, *Breakfast at Tiffany's* (New York: Random House, 1958), p. 3.

19. William L. Nance, *The Worlds of Truman Capote* (New York: Stein & Day, 1973), p. 123.
20. Donald R. Noble, 'The Future of Southern Writing', p. 579.
21. Barry Hannah, *Ray* (New York: Penguin Books, 1981), p. 3.
22. J. H. E. Paine, *Theory and Criticism of the Novella*, p. 124.
23. Robert Boyers, *Atrocity and Amnesia: The Political Novel Since 1945* (New York and Oxford: Oxford University Press, 1985), p. 4.
24. Anne Goodwyn Jones, *Tomorrow is Another Day: The Woman Writer in the South 1859–1936* (Baton Rouge & London: Louisiana State University Press, 1981), p. 37.
25. Anne Goodwyn Jones, '*Gone With the Wind* and Others: Popular Fiction 1920 to 1950', in *The History of Southern Literature*, p. 364.
26. *Tomorrow is Another Day*, p. 39. Given the 'tradition of women's silence' (ibid., p. 39) in the public life of the South, fiction becomes a way of overcoming the barriers between private thought and public utterance.
27. Though this is perhaps explained by the chronological limits of her study, and the changes which have occurred in the concerns of Southern women's writing since 1936. Is there, one might ask, an earlier (chronological) abandonment of concern with any kind of 'public truths' on the part of the female writer than the male? Certainly, Richard King (p. 9) notes a relative unconcern 'with larger cultural, racial, and political themes' on the part of women writers which such a patterning would endorse. Any such speculation must remain highly tentative.
28. One might speculate that the modernist tradition, in which most of the writers I have examined are working, is by and large, suspicious of the public voice and of the social 'problem' as fit subject for fiction. This could go towards explaining such an absence.
29. Katherine Anne Porter, *Old Mortality*, in *Pale Horse, Pale Rider: Three Short Novels* (New York: Modern Library, 1949), p. 39.
30. *Old Mortality*, p. 88. The final ambiguity of response to Miranda's rebellion is textually marked by the shift from first to third person voice which occurs in mid-sentence right at the end of the novella.
31. See *The Leaning Tower and Other Stories* (New York: Harcourt, Brace and Company, 1944), pp. 166–67. In this novella, Porter does take on consciously historical themes but in a European context and, noticeably, through the use of a central protagonist who is male.
32. *Tomorrow is Another Day*, pp. 10 and 11.
33. *Tomorrow is Another Day*, pp. 45 and 42.
34. Eudora Welty, *The Ponder Heart* (New York: Harcourt, Brace and Co., 1954), p. 116.
35. Peggy Whitman Prenshaw, 'Eudora Welty', in *The History of Southern Literature*, p. 473.
36. Ruth M. Vande Kieft, *Eudora Welty* (New York: Twayne Publishers, Inc., 1962), pp. 71 and 173. It should be pointed out that it is possible to read Welty's text ironically, focusing on the gap between Edna's wit and the witlessness of Daniel, who she spends her whole life caring for and protecting. This might be seen as ironic comment on the waste of a woman's talents and individuality, in a culture which confines females to

such protective and mothering rôles. Because the text is first-person, however, such a reading cannot be explicitly signalled.

37. Oliver Evans, *Carson McCullers: Her Life and Work* (London: Peter Owen, 1965), p. 131.

38. Carson McCullers, *The Ballad of the Sad Café* (Harmondsworth, Middlesex: Penguin Books, 1963), p. 66.

39. Amelia's sexual unease is clearly signalled in the text and related to her relationship with her father. It is realized not only in her behaviour on her wedding night, but also in her 'doctoring': 'if a patient came with a female complaint, she could do nothing. Indeed, at the mere mention of the words her face would slowly darken with shame' (p. 23).

40. Donald R. Noble, 'The Future of Southern Writing', and Martha E. Cook, 'Old Ways and New Ways', both in *The History of Southern Literature*, pp. 578 and 534.

8

Keeping it in the Family: The Novellas of J. D. Salinger

by DAVID SEED

In contrast with the extensive critical attention devoted to *The Catcher in the Rye* the novellas of J.D. Salinger have, with very few exceptions, either been greeted with silence or disapproval. They have been attacked for being 'hopelessly prolix' (Irving Howe), the products of 'an impersonator of adolescence' (Leslie Fiedler), the result of contradiction since 'Salinger can . . . exercise his art with reverence, while still despising the "culture" which makes it possible' (Frank Kermode), or the result of lost detachment since Salinger 'identifies himself too fussily with the spiritual aches and pains of his characters' (Alfred Kazin).[1] More recently Malcolm Bradbury has argued that Salinger's efforts in these novellas to break through the unavoidable deceits of fiction almost destroy the narrative.[2]

In these attacks there is a consensus that Salinger had lost the critical detachment necessary to view his characters—and especially Seymour Glass—objectively, but in what follows I shall be arguing that the creation of the Glass family as a whole enables Salinger to use a variety of narrative methods which he might otherwise not have had available to him. For the family structure becomes crucial in the definition of his characters and even makes it possible for Salinger to incorporate the reader's anticipated criticisms into his own narrative. Salinger himself evidently viewed his own fictional family with relish for when *Raise High the Roof Beam, Carpenters* and *Seymour—An Introduction* were published together in book form he declared on the dust-jacket that 'the joys and satisfactions of working on the Glass family peculiarly increase and deepen for me with the years.'[3] It is a relish, however, which has not kept him free of repetition or a certain tortuous self-consciousness.

Salinger's first published novellas, *The Inverted Forest* (1947) and *Franny* (1955), both deal with examples of failed self-realization, but use diametrically opposed methods. *The Inverted Forest* differs markedly from his '50s novellas in covering a considerable timespan (1917–37) through an intermittent narrative. The protagonist, Corinne von Nordhoffen, notes in her diary that she loves and intends to marry a boy called Ray Ford. The opening childhood scenes show Corinne's birthday-party (ruined by Ray's non-appearance) and the eviction of Ray and his mother from their apartment. Ray drops out of Corinne's life for twenty years, during which time she jealously guards the privacy of her memories in spite of the perception of one of her dates ('When he found out just how regularly Corinne was making private trips back to her childhood, he tried to do something about it. With the best intentions he tried to set up some kind of detour in Corinne's mind')[4]. His sudden and ludicrous death prevents the 'detour' from materializing, and Corinne makes a successful career for herself on a New York magazine. Coming across some of Ray Ford's poems one day, she arranges a meeting, starts dating him and—in spite of warnings to the contrary—marries him. There now enters the third character in this triangle, an aspiring poet called Mary Croft who brings some of her pieces to New York for Ray to read. Unbeknown to Corinne, they start an affair and run away together. The narrative closes with Corinne's unsuccessful attempt to reclaim her husband.

Salinger's use of a limited point of view, namely Corinne's, is then actually phrased in the third person which implies an alternative perspective without spelling it out. One such implication, for instance, is that Corinne builds up her romantic hopes to fill the void in her personal life whose routine is summarized as a mock-office memorandum shortly before Ray Ford reappears.

In fact Salinger makes considerable play of absences, hiatuses and interruptions in this novella to reveal Corinne's sense of value (her office career pales into insignificance before her 'romance') and then to demonstrate the failure of her love. Physical absence—introduced in the early scene of flawed domesticity at Corinne's birthday party—becomes the central theme of this novella where romantic yearning degenerates finally into an undignified and fruitless pursuit. If Corinne's desires become the expression of emotional need, it is yet another irony to this bleak narrative that she should look to a neurotic for satisfaction. Salinger glances repeatedly at Ray Ford's erratic behaviour, his terrifying nightmares and increasing alcoholism, to suggest that he is not in control of his own actions and never responsive to Corinne's overtures. The stylistic expression of this emotional distance is the pointed formality which the narrator adopts in the second half of the novella. Take, for example, the final meeting between the Fords after Ray has inexplicably failed to arrive during the evening:

> At approximately four A.M., having twice walked completely around the block, Mrs. Ford encountered Mr. Ford under the canopy of their apartment house as he was getting out of a taxi. He was wearing a new hat. Mrs. Ford said hello to Mr. Ford and asked him where did he get the hat. Mr. Ford did not seem to hear the question.[5]

The use of what is described as a 'private detective's log' for enumerating actions sets up a gap between Corinne's implied feelings and what is registered in the description. Salinger offers details such as Ford's purchase of his new hat to suggest that there is another action going on elsewhere. If Ford would not take the trouble to dress well for his wife, then who is appreciating the new hat?

As its title suggests, *The Inverted Forest* turns romance and domesticity on their heads. Even Salinger's choice of a name for his protagonist plays its part here, possibly drawing on Madame de Staël's romantic novel *Corinne* (1807) where the eponymous heroine, herself a poetess, holds back from committing herself to the lord she loves and ultimately dies of grief when he marries her half-sister. By retaining this name Salinger points to the grand passions and tragic romantic destiny which are *not* available to his Corinne. In his novella romance is constantly deflated, reduced to absurdity and denied any resolving glamour. *The Inverted Forest* repeatedly reverses romance and domesticity, presenting their absence as farce or black comedy. After Ray and Mary run away together 'Miss' Croft's husband appears at Corinne's apartment, explains that his marriage has been failing, and then tries to proposition Corinne! When Corinne finally tracks down the two fugitives in a mid-Western city her visit takes on a bizarre tone from the constant observation of social courtesies. Not only has the original situation of Mary's visit reversed, but there is no recognition that Ray is Corinne's husband. She rings their bell 'casually, like a salesman or a friend', and the subsequent scene confirms the analogies. This technique of understatement effectively isolates Corinne within a series of events which resemble a comic nightmare. Mary Croft's husband actually reinforces one of the novella's most pointed implications (of Corinne's self-ignorance) when he presents to her an appallingly hearty visiting card which reads: 'I'M HOWIE CROFT. Who the Hell are you, Bud?' When Corinne leaves her husband's new apartment she runs off into night, physically enacting her search for an identity which the novella as a whole has suggested she will never find.

The Inverted Forest exemplifies a category of novella identified by Mary Doyle Springer as 'degenerative or pathetic tragedy' which 'consists in the relentless, relatively simple [in plot], and swift degeneration of a central character into unrelieved misery or death'.⁶ Salinger's irony excludes tragedy but retains the degenerative pattern. This pattern emerges through narrative hints, through the use of scenic comment and parallelism (Corinne's visit to her husband's flat repeats Mary's visit to her own), and also through narrative concealment. Salinger's hints direct the reader towards what is *not* disclosed even more than to what is evident on the narrative surface, and this exploitation of a subtext becomes crucial in Salinger's next novella, *Franny*.

With *Franny* Salinger changes his conception of length entirely. *The Inverted Forest* reads at points like a compressed novel, summarizing events of secondary importance so as to narrate the whole fate of its protagonist. For his second novella Salinger contracts the span of the action into a few hours, yet extends their duration by brilliantly exploiting every physical detail and nuance of speech. The location is almost entirely one scene in a restaurant; the occasion is the beginning of a weekend date between two students (Franny and Lane). Where the narrative ironies of *The Inverted Forest* revolve partly around movement from place to place, gesture now assumes importance. Where romance is firmly inverted or blocked (there is no correlation between Ray's poetry and his rôle as lover, for instance) at the expense of any feeling other than panic, Salinger now investigates romantic disappointment with far greater psychological subtlety. Franny's feelings do not follow a trajectory of high hopes being followed by disappointment. What is much more threatening to her is routine, the slippage of her emotions and desires into clichéd patterns.

The narrative begins with a group scene, specifically a group of male students waiting for their dates to arrive by train. Lane stands to one side as if to define himself against the group, but Salinger is careful to state that 'he was and he wasn't one of them.' This apparent paradox really raises a question about the limitations of Lane's individuality. Throughout his writings Salinger shows an acute sensitivity to social cliché and stereotype, sometimes allowing characters to take on substance only after they have been registered as, for instance, 'the gray-haired man' or 'the girl' (in 'Pretty Mouth and Green my Eyes' (1951)). In the case of Lane, Salinger intermittently reminds the reader that he is either typical or likely to conform to typical rôles. Even the lunch which he eats with Franny in Sickler's restaurant is the latest in a series of dates. Unlike Lane, Franny explicitly identifies a number of social types even while she is herself conforming to a typical situation. The girls she has seen on the train and the section men (i.e. students who stand in for tutors) she has described all fit into ironically clear categories, to the annoyance of Lane since she even pluralizes his friend Wally Campbell into a type (Wally Campbells being tiresome name-droppers). Franny's attitude comes to resemble the ironic detachment of the overall narrative voice, but not without physical and emotional cost.

One urgency established in the novella is her efforts to salvage her identity, to prevent herself from becoming a cliché. Hence the recurring pattern in her utterances of critical assertions being followed by waves of revulsion against herself.

When Franny tells Lane that she has abandoned a play she was acting in, the text alerts us to a possible histrionic dimension in Salinger's own characters' behaviour. The first conversation in the restaurant is presented in terms of style not content, the latter being almost completely excluded. The following passage is typical:

> Lane was speaking now as someone does who has been monop-olizing conversation for a good quarter of an hour or so. . . . He was slouched rhetorically forward, toward Franny, his receptive audience, a supporting forearm on either side of his Martini.[7]

Even Lane's body is rendered theatrically as if his torso were a leading actor and his arms the supporting cast. Franny is a cap-tive audience within a conversation where the participants wait their turn to deliver monologues. The quotation also demon-strates a crucial change in perspective between this work and Salinger's first novella. In *The Inverted Forest* Salinger implicitly demonstrates that Corinne is the foolish victim of her own romantic hopes. Here the ostensible narrative tone is once again impassive, but in fact Salinger's comparison between Lane's posture and a type ('as someone does who . . .') suggests that the narrator is endorsing Franny's own critical insights into typical patterns of behaviour. Indeed, the sense of social behaviour as theatre is everywhere present in *Franny*, emerging through the vocabulary of simulations and semblances. The repeated ways in which Franny and Lane arrange their features so as to play their parts more efficiently, and through such ironies as Franny searching for her obligatory 'lines' after she faints.

Franny has decided to abandon acting when she was backstage, and Salinger also takes us 'backstage' with his protagonist in a number of ways. Franny's revulsion from the patterns of social behaviour defamiliarizes the novella's central situation—a lunch—and transforms it into an exercise of tactics, a psychological struggle between the two participants. Her opposition to Lane emerges partly through her refusal to play out the rôle of a weekend date being wined and dined by her boyfriend, so that she orders a chicken sandwich instead of the restaurant's famous snails. Thwarted from acting out the rôle he has been expecting, Lane exploits his anger to try to force conformity on Franny—but with no success. Her answers to questions are less than satisfactory ('No, Yes and no. I don't know') and the distance between the two characters widens, Franny watching Lane 'as if he were a stranger, or a poster advertising a brand of linoleum, across the aisle of a subway car' (p. 19). As speech and behaviour become divorced from feeling, Franny's anxieties increase and she seeks refuge in the ladies' room. This withdrawal (she sits in a foetal position) and obliteration of visual perception into a 'voidlike black' is a moment of intense privacy, and Salinger grants us a unique access to her temporary breakdown just as we also gain significant access to her consciousness (Lane's few recorded thoughts are sometimes phrased as hypotheses). Since the use of language in society for Franny is tainted with inauthenticity, then Salinger seems to be setting up an extra-social perspective on Franny.

Unlike the vernacular of *The Catcher in the Rye* (whose careful blend of slang, borrowings from the movies, etc. implies a social group containing Holden and the implied reader), the narrator of *Franny* uses a scrupulously neutral register which contrasts ironically with Lane's idiom. Through this neutral but not unsolicitous language Salinger presents Franny's gradual collapse. The physical symptoms (trembling, nausea, etc.) are clear enough, but even chance remarks ('I look like a ghost') reinforce the sombre theme of Franny's disintegrating identity. Like Holden Caulfield she imagines her own disappearance and experiences waves of vertigo. It should by now have become clear what an enormous gap there is between the novella's ostensible and actual subjects. On the surface Salinger is presenting a weekend date, but beneath the realistic surface he is dramatizing a critical point in a character's breakdown. At this point we should turn to the novella's psychological dimension.

In a long and detailed Freudian reading of *Franny* Daniel Seitzman exposes what he calls the 'psychodynamics' of the work.[8] He locates beneath the surface of the text a struggle for sexual supremacy between Franny and Lane, so that, whatever subject they may be discussing, there is always a deeper and more intense drama going on which becomes more and more evident as the narrative progresses. In summary 'the more Lane tries to prove that he truly possesses the male organ the more Franny tries to prove that he is just as deficient as she.' Seitzman's analysis is particularly useful for drawing our attention to the implications of physical gesture and utterance, and also to the combative logic to the dialogues in the novella which carry from monologue to attack and defence. He is certainly right that Salinger uses speech as part of psychological tactics, and right too that the letter from Franny which Lane reads consists of thinly veiled sexual threats. Thus she writes: 'I hate you when you're being hopelessly super-male and reticent. Not really *hate* you but am constitutionally against strong, silent men. Not that you aren't strong . . .' (p. 10). Hatred and sexual opposition are glossed over by her as charming gaffs, but Franny gives Lane (and the reader) his lead by inviting him to analyze the letter.

Psycho-analysis is a slippery and ambiguous topic in Salinger's fiction. On the one hand (and here his fiction blends entirely into the *New Yorker* ethos of the 1940s and 1950s), it is routinely the subject of ironic jokes. On the other, Salinger clearly builds psycho-analytical subtleties into his fiction, especially the longer works of the fifties. As Seitzman notes, Lane claims not to be a 'Freudian man' in explicating literature, but he then proceeds to act as an amateur psychoanalyst. This activity is complicated by the fact that he is not a disinterested party so that his amateur psycho-analysis becomes part of the overt narrative content, masking his drive for sexual supremacy. After Franny faints she comes to on the couch of the manager's office, i.e. in the posture of a patient undergoing psychoanalysis. Lane then opportunistically uses her passivity to insist on his sexual rights to her, once again partly camouflaging this pressure as concern for her physical welfare. In a sense Lane has won at the end of the novella since Franny is now entirely at his disposal, passively submissive to his plans for the rest of the day.

The one buffer against collapse which Franny carries around with her is a slim volume entitled *The Way of a Pilgrim*. Seitzman's argument would assimilate this text into Salinger's psychological themes, relating it to Franny's repressions. Given the context of allusions to psychoanalysis, it is impossible not to see the book (and the Jesus prayer it contains) in therapeutic terms. However, to do so implicates the reader in the discredited tactics of Lane and goes against the perspective of the novella itself. If Franny defines the measure of importance, then we obviously need to pin down the book's significance for her flight from self-consciousness. *The Way of a Pilgrim* is an anonymous nineteenth-century narrative of spiritual searching by a Russian who travels around the country trying to attach clear meaning to the injunction in I. Thessalonians v, 17, 'pray without ceasing'. Formally *The Way of the Pilgrim* contrasts strikingly with *Franny* in many respects. It is a travel-narrative where Franny herself is relatively immobile; it is punctuated by moments of insight and the seeker is guided by a religious sage, whereas Franny's insights are ambivalent, incoherent and solitary; it is also a text about *using* texts since the pilgrim carries a manual of prayer with him (*The Philokalia*), and a text for use itself, although Franny retreats behind agnosticism in the face of Lane's attacks. The particular episode which Franny describes is a meal-time scene where the pilgrim is welcomed with great hospitality. There is an obvious enough contrast here between the one scene and the situation in Salinger's novella, where Lane interrupts Franny's account by commenting on the frog's legs he is eating.

These intertextual ironies underline the pathos of Franny's predicament, and the Jesus prayer surely tantalizes her by suggesting a way in which words can be once again joined to meaning. The pilgrim's guide (the *starets*) tells him:

> Carry your mind, i.e. your thoughts from your head to your heart . . . As you breathe out, say 'Lord Jesus Christ, have mercy on me'. Say it moving your lips gently, or simply say it in your mind.[9]

The prayer is partly about reforming the connections (head to heart, words to truth) which have broken in Franny's case. What fascinates her is the possibility that certain words or even a name 'has this peculiar, self-active power of its own' (p. 34). Where she is trying to resacralize words (to use them repetitively as a kind of mantra), to Lane 'God' is only available as an exclamation. Salinger carefully refuses to be explicit over Franny's degree of success here. When she moves her lips at the end of the novella, there is a clear allusion to the Jesus prayer. But equally well Franny could have lapsed into silent withdrawal.

When *Franny* was published in book form with a companion novella, *Zooey*, John Updike shrewdly pointed out that the volume presented *two* Frannies—one without a background, and one related to the Glass family.[10] This change marks a crucial turning-point in Salinger's career. From now on the family takes on major importance in determining the kinds of narrative he constructs and the kinds of relations available to his characters. *Franny* as a separate novella gains a lot of force from the isolation of its protagonist from any kind of family context. Partly this is a question of Franny's lack of support which increases her vulnerability to Lane's psychological bullying; partly it reflects the novella's emphasis on the present, on the moment-by-moment developments within the immediate situation. When the novella is revised into a family context, Franny is given a past and our view of her changes considerably. The introduction of the Glass family was not an entirely new phenomenon in Salinger's career. As early as 1941 Salinger was considering writing stories about the members of a family—this time the Caulfields—and he subsequently published two narratives ('Last Day of the Last Furlough', (1944) and 'This Sandwich has no Mayonnaise' (1945)) dealing with Holden Caulfield's brothers. Through the 1940s Salinger considered assembling his Caulfield stories into a sequence, but chose instead to incorporate at least two previously published sketches into *The Catcher in the Rye*, which was published in 1951 but which had originally been completed in 1946 as a ninety-page novella.[11]

The first dramatization of a member of the Glass family occurs in the story 'A Perfect Day for Bananafish' (1948), in which Seymour commits suicide. This carefully constructed piece tantalizingly hints at Seymour's behaviour through comments made during a telephone conversation between his wife Muriel and her mother. The latter cryptically refers to 'funny business' or 'the business with the window', although Muriel under-reacts throughout. In her, nonchalance is taken to the point of indifference, suggesting within the first few pages of the story a possible clash of character between husband and wife. The second section, where Seymour chats to a little girl on the beach, raises a second problem in the implied disparity between childish innocence and a near-paranoid sensitivity to other adults, a disparity which informs most of Salinger's fiction.

Two points need stressing here. One is that Salinger first imagined Seymour as a suicide; in the subsequent Glass family novellas he becomes an absent character, a figure who usually precedes the specific narrative. Secondly 'A Perfect Day' conforms to a pattern of well-made short stories published in such journals as the *New Yorker* or *Esquire* in the 1940s and early 1950s which use a dispassionate narrative voice and which conclude with an ironic twist. Seymour's suicide is an understated event which startles the reader and throws him back into the text to look for symptoms. But not much will be discovered because the story's very brevity minimizes information and maximizes the suicide's final impact. Once the suicide has been assimilated into the Glass family mythology a longer narrative form is needed so that the members of that family can ruminate over this appalling event. Seymour (and specifically Seymour's death) becomes a crucial reference-point within the Glass family.

Franny demonstrates several characteristics of Salinger's early stories in spite of its length: the generalized scene-setting, playing off one character against another, the suggestion of imminent crisis and the ambivalent ending. Once seen as a companion piece to *Zooey*, however, it is given a past and sequel; in other words, it becomes relocated within a longer narrative sequence. Even Franny's psychology changes. What emerged initially as a general revulsion from social hypocrisy becomes revised into a specific consequence of Seymour's influence over Franny. The question of identity which Howard Nemerov sees as crucial to the novella form also undergoes revision. Nemerov states that

> the mutual attachment or dependency between A and B [the 'agonists' of the novella] has a mortal strength; its dissolution requires a crisis fatal to one or the other party; but this dissolution is required as salvation.[12]

The application of this generalization to the psychological struggle between Franny and Lane is clear enough.

In *Zooey* the eponymous protagonist replaces Lane as an *anta*gonist, this time with reference to a figure no longer present—to Seymour. Zooey himself makes this replacement explicit (and strengthens links with the preceding novella) by attacking Lane but also takes on Franny's earlier rôle by explaining the meaning and origin of *The Way of a Pilgrim*. His conversations with Franny take up where the first novella left

149

off, since she is again lying on a couch in the posture of a patient. Partly for this reason Daniel Seitzman sees the conversations as 'sessions' where Zooey tries to break down the armour of Franny's identifications, using techniques which are so blatant that they are antitherapeutic.[13] Once again he demonstrates Salinger's psychological subtlety with the difference now that Zooey is well aware what he is doing. The attacks on Franny are all the more telling because they are skilfully directed at vulnerable areas of her adopted piety; Zooey charges her with escapism, sentimentality and spiritual acquisitiveness, making an oddly old-fashioned appeal to duty. He is careful to distinguish his actions from the normalizing procedures of Freudian analysis. Addressing his mother he declares:

> You just call in some analyst who's experienced in adjusting people to the joys of television, and *Life* magazine every Wednesday, and European travel, and the H-Bomb . . . and I swear to you, in not more than a year Franny'll either be in a *nut* ward or she'll be wandering off into some goddam desert with a burning cross in her hands. (p. 88)

Zooey's ironic recitation of all the 'gloriously normal' factors of American life in the mid-'50s suggests a disengagement, a standing off from stereotyped patterns of social behaviour. He is well aware that even piety can fall into these grooves, mocking his mother's dismay that religion might involve inconvenience through a side-swipe at the application of marketing techniques to personality-development by such figures as Norman Vincent Peale.[14]

Our sense of the apartment as a home is crucial here. In *The Catcher in the Rye* Holden's return to his parents' apartment is ambiguous. It cannot function as a refuge, nevertheless it tugs him back; he pays a visit, but almost like a thief since he is only seen by his younger sister Phoebe. In *Zooey* the detailed description of the contents of the family medicine cabinet, of bookshelves and furnishings, becomes an important part of the novella's rhetoric. Buddy describes the living-room as 'a kind of visual hymn to commercial American childhood and early puberty' (p. 97) and states that the furnishings were 'old, intrinsically unlovely, and clotted with memory and sentiment' (p. 98). The slow enumeration of details—purple passages because the sheer detail constantly overwhelms whatever is locally necessary—becomes a means of indicating the past. In an odd and rather cloying way the Glass apartment resembles a private museum dedicated to the vaudeville career of Les and Bessie, and to the memory of their children's intellectual precocity. When Bessie waxes nostalgic over the years when the children were all together, she is making explicit an emotional undercurrent in Salinger's depiction of their apartment. Similarly Les Glass (one of the most shadowy members of the family), we are told, lives entirely in the past, his one function in this novella being to reminisce over the old days with Franny. The many references to theatre do not at all function like similar references in *Franny* where the reader is invited to consider patterns in behaviour, but are rather assimilated into the family's collective history. They become a means of cementing domestic solidarity because they include Les and Bessie's career, the children's performance on a radio quiz show called 'It's a Wise Child' (no doubt based on an actual show from the '30s called 'Quiz Kids'), and Zooey's present occupation as actor. In the conversations between Zooey and his mother and Zooey and Franny, there is always present an element of the histrionic and appreciation by one speaker of the other's style. While Zooey and Franny may be jockeying for the leading rôle (Zooey says at one point, 'I hate like hell to play Martha to somebody else's Mary' (p. 125)), this rôle is constantly swinging from one to the other as they engage in performances for each other's benefit.

A family is by definition a collective structure of relations, one which can be revealed in fiction by one member talking about another. It is a common tactic in Faulkner's fiction, for instance, for characters to be placed through such 'relating' terms as 'cousin' or 'uncle'. The implied approval between the narrator's intelligence and Franny's view of society in her novella changes into an altogether more explicit relation in *Zooey* where the narrator is named as Buddy Glass, her brother. Immediately our earlier impression of Franny's existential isolation is lost, especially as the sources of information multiply to include Zooey and their mother Bessie Glass. Subject-matter becomes more and more introverted as the members of the Glass family discuss themselves. Now the danger is that Salinger will not multiply points of view rendering problematic the existence of a family structure (as happens in *The Sound and the Fury*) but that he will create a mutual admiration society. Whatever incidental humour the opening conversation of *Zooey* may carry (fussy mother vs. sophisticated and long-suffering son), it also enables the reader to start building up a picture of the family. Narrative comments help this process because they interpret physical reactions on an implied basis of long familiarity ('. . . a flicker came into her eyes—no more than a flicker, but a flicker—of connoisseur like, if perverse, relish for her youngest, and only handsome, son's style of bullying' (p. 68)). The detailed description of Zooey's ablutions (he is taking a bath at the beginning of the novella) does not define him dramatically against another character (as in *Franny*), but draws out his actions as part of a gradual revelation of the Glass family. It is the family which is the real subject, the real focus of attention, and one which absorbs Franny's breakdown into a much broader context.

If the Glass family is a unit, it is a unit without some of its main members. Curiously, as with his planned Caulfield sequence, Salinger only decided to use the family after its leading member had been killed off. When Buddy begins his narrative, he admits that of the seven Glass children 'the senior five will be stalking in and out of the plot with considerable frequency, like so many Banquo's ghosts' (p. 47). In spite of their physical absence Seymour and Buddy exert an important pressure throughout the narrative, so much so that Zooey exclaims against them: 'this whole goddam house stinks of ghosts' (p. 84). If the apartment is haunted, then one way in which Franny's cure could be seen is as a coming to terms with the ghost of Seymour. So when Zooey enters Seymour's bedroom towards the end of the novella, the tone becomes appropriately reverential as if Zooey has entered a shrine. Once again the narrative is slowed down so that the angle of vision can pan round the room registering Seymour's desk and his collage of quotations from world literature. Zooey in effect steps back into the past just as Franny is transformed back into a child as she sleeps ('as though, at twenty, she had chucked back into the mute, fisty defenses of the nursery' (p. 99)), and as she enters her parents' bedroom when her dressing gown 'looked as if it had been changed into a small child's woollen bathrobe' (p. 146). Having both regressed into the past it is appropriate that Zooey's piece of therapeutic wisdom to Franny about the Fat lady (a composite audience—and fantasy-figure) should come from the dead Seymour.[15] This novella has been attacked repeatedly for being too garrulous, Warren French complaining that 'the author *talks* too much and *shows* too little', but that is not the main problem.[16] Salinger slows down and elongates his narrative so that he can extract the maximum relish out of his cherished Glass family. The length of the novella now offers Salinger the opportunity to savour the gradual release of narrative information, not to unfold a drama, but to build up a picture of the past. The Glass family supplies narrative means (Buddy), leading characters (Zooey and Bessie), subject (Franny) and privileged reference-point (Seymour); thus the family engrosses all the formal aspects of its own narrative. Even an outsider's view of the children as intellectual freaks is assimilated into the family's collective self-consciousness, and this to a certain extent is defused as criticism.

Another critical problem in Salinger's use of the Glass family is that it blurs the boundary of each text and constantly hints at significant events having taken place before the specific narratives begin. The significance of these events has to be taken on trust because the reader is given no direct or impartial access to them. Unfortunately the development of the Glass series has gone hand in hand with the gradual inflation of Seymour into a failed god-seeker. Eberhard Alsen, the only critic to examine the notion of series in any detail, has described the narratives as a 'composite novel about Seymour's life and his teachings'.[17] He sees the guiding principle behind the series as an inspirational theory of art and makes no bones about placing Seymour as leading character. The works are linked, he continues, partly through Buddy's narrative voice and partly through what he calls 'shared references'; i.e. certain key events in the Glass history, most notably Seymour's suicide, which become common points of reference for the Glass novellas. Significantly Seymour's suicide only takes on its portentous significance once Salinger started developing his series. It is never described in the series, only alluded to constantly. Alsen's reading of the Glass series simply accepts Seymour's piety at face value and says little about the rhetorical tactics Salinger uses to convince us of his stature. It is one thing to find a continuity from novella to novella and quite another to reduce all their issues to the single problem of Seymour's stature, which is anyway not constant.

Raise High the Roofbeams, Carpenter falls between *Franny* and *Zooey* in the sense that Seymour is taking on importance but has not yet been transformed into a sage. Like *Franny* it has a naturalistic structure—a segment of Seymour's wedding day in 1942. When he does not appear for the ceremony, the guests disperse in the hired cars. Buddy (the narrator) finds himself squeezed between a Mrs. Silsbury, a benign dwarf who turns out to be a deaf-mute, and the Matron of Honor and her husband. Held up in the New York traffic, Buddy leads them to the Glass children's apartment and supplies them with drinks. When they hear that Seymour and Muriel have eloped, the guests leave. Buddy narrates these events in an ironically distanced tone which concentrates humorously on the variety of reactions to Seymour's non-appearance. In this narrative his absence acts as a comic stimulus to the indignation of the guests, specifically that of the Matron of Honor who attacks Seymour most vociferously. Partly to delay the revelation of his own identity Buddy maintains his silence through these attacks, only 'answering back' through his narrative comments: her stare 'seemed to come from a one-woman mob'.[18] He actually argues with her once he has been fortified with alcohol.

Throughout this novella a dialogue is going on between the Matron of Honor's bullying version of normality and Buddy's general defence of his brother. In that sense *Raise High* restates in comic form the themes of *Franny* where psychological conflict is replaced by temporary disguise. Buddy uses silence to delay revealing his identity, but nothing worse than physical discomfort is at stake for him—certainly not breakdown. Where Franny would like to withdraw from all social forms, Buddy fills the gap left by Seymour to act as host to the others. *Raise High* skilfully balances internal and external views of the Glass family, which suggests that Seymour's status has not yet been fixed, but that it is still a matter of one perspective playing against its opposite. Seymour's piety in *Zooey* has yet to come.

Apart from its situational comedy *Raise High* also devotes a lot of attention to the transmission of information between the members of the Glass family. Once again the effect is to prevent Seymour's significance from being fixed. Buddy's rôle is thus both verbal (as narrator) and transmissive in the sense that he collects the various Glass communications and conveys them to the reader—from his sister Boo Boo's letter about the marriage through to the messages scrawled on the mirror in Buddy's flat to the excerpts he reads from Seymour's diary. The immediate narrative of the characters' movements through the streets of New York foreshadows the diary excerpts in several respects: they are halted by a parade while Seymour's excerpts begin with a parade; his criticism by Mrs. Fedder (his fiancée's mother) have been anticipated by the Matron of Honor, and so on. Temporarily Seymour takes over as narrator giving *his* version of himself, a psychoanalysis of Muriel and declarations of love which conflict implicitly with his casual criticism of her ('Her marital goals are so absurd and touching').

In spite of being a diary, i.e. a day-to-day narrative, Seymour's account is mostly phrased in the past tense and as such is retrospective. Seymour's account thus joins other accounts in this novella which is ultimately about an enigma. Buddy's narrative is carefully dated at 1955, about 1942 (and he constantly reminds the reader of his youthful naïveté at that time). Seymour's narrative is dated 1941 to 1942, i.e. the months leading up to his marriage. But between the novella's time of action (1942) and time of narration (1955) Buddy has thrown out an intervening date: 1948, the year of Seymour's suicide. In other words, the reader knows about Seymour's fate long before he hears that he has not appeared for his marriage. After Buddy closes Seymour's diary we hear that Seymour and Muriel have eloped. This reads like a romantic resolution but is complicated by Buddy's (and the reader's) knowledge of his death. At the beginning of *Raise High* Buddy recounts a Taoist tale which Seymour had read to Franny when she was very young. It is a parable on perception where a character named Kao is described as follows: 'In making sure of the essential, he forgets the homely details; intent on the inward qualities, he loses sight of the external' (p. 5). Buddy carefully refuses to disclose why he retells this tale—it is certainly not just to supply biographical data about Seymour. The tale, then, is introduced as an enigma and in that respect anticipates the enigmatic qualities of Seymour himself. The crux of the tale is to distinguish between incidental and essential qualities.

By stressing how young and confused he was in 1942 Buddy surely implies that he himself was incapable of drawing such distinctions at that time. Might he not have missed some tell-tale signs in Seymour's diary, for instance, which would explain the mystery of his suicide? *Raise High* seems to be about romantic beginnings but varies its narrative means (having a story within the story and briefly a narrator within a narrator) to raise questions about Seymour's puzzling end.

The development in narrative method from *Franny* through the four subsequent novellas also reflects a growing introversion. *Franny* is recounted by an anonymous self-effacing narrator. *Raise High* introduces Buddy as both narrator and protagonist, but with relatively few asides. In *Zooey* (1957) Buddy offers the reader what he calls a 'prose home movie', implicitly made by the family for its own consumption. He anticipates objections to his own narrative by recasting characters (Bessie, Franny, Zooey) as critics and demonstrates a far-greater self-consciousness about the processes of narration and the verbosity of his own style. In *Seymour—An Introduction* (1959) this self-consciousness reaches its maximum. Plot and narrative sequence give way to a monologue on writing. Bernice and Sanford Goldstein have described this work rightly as a 'fictional treatise on the artistic process', although 'treatise' sounds rather heavy to describe Salinger's ruminating and often playful prose style.[19]

As the title of the piece suggests, Salinger is particularly concerned with beginnings, hence his preliminary skirmishings with the 'general reader' and with the then modish image of the writer as neurotic. The preamble shows Salinger trying to avoid such images and labels, and trying too to avoid any connections with Beat Literature.[20] It becomes increasingly evident that notional distinctions between Buddy as narrator and Salinger himself must break down from the narrator's unmistakable allusions to *The Catcher in the Rye* and to himself as a famous writer. Salinger simultaneously invites the reader to view his statements as directly confessional but sets up a theatrical screen of verbiage where Fieldingesque digressions and agile shifts of narrative posture prevent any sustained self-image from taking shape. John O. Lyons has compared these tactics with the self-conscious Romantic style of Byron's *Don Juan*. He notes:

The Novellas of J. D. Salinger

In every case there is a difference between the writer and the narrator or hero, but the reader is constantly teased with the similarities between the historical writer and his professional mask or his hero.[21]

Seymour now becomes the personification of a fictional subject, the focus and origin of formal problems of expression. Salinger genially makes it clear why he has abandoned the tightly knit short-story form of his early career using fictive gestures reminiscent of the opening of *Lolita*:

> . . . on this occasion I'm anything but a short-story writer where my brother is concerned. What I am, I think, is a thesaurus of undetached prefatory remarks about him. I believe I essentially remain what I've almost always been—a narrator, but one with extremely pressing personal needs. I want to introduce, I want to describe, I want to distribute mementos, amulets, I want to break out my wallet and pass around snapshots, I want to follow my nose. In this mood, I don't dare go anywhere near the short-story form. It eats up fat little undetached writers like me whole. (p. 125)

Salinger humorously identifies himself literally with his own words so that he becomes a disembodied voice, a series of verbal constructs so expansive that he needs the extra space of the novella form. In effect he realizes a fear he expressed on the dust-jacket of *Franny and Zooey*: 'there is a real-enough danger, I suppose, that sooner or later I'll bog down, perhaps disappear entirely, in my own methods, locutions, and mannerisms.'

In *Seymour—An Introduction* these mannerisms are foregrounded so that their expression becomes the main narrative. Whereas in *Franny* gaps in the text corresponded to passages of time where nothing important was happening (going from the station to the restaurant, for instance), now the text is ostentatiously interrupted so that the 'author' can get his much-needed sleep. Ihab Hassan has generalized this verbal self-consciousness into a characteristic of all of Salinger's novellas which 'makes use of all the resources of language, including accident, or distortion, to convey an unmediated vision of reality'. Hassan locates the main theme of this particular novella as a justification of language 'which must, in the same breath, try and fail to encompass holiness'.[22] The difficulties and ultimate failure of narrative does indeed become the subject of *Seymour—An Introduction*.

Although Salinger lays down a credo about the value of the artist-seer at the end of his preamble, the true progression to his 'introduction' is a rhythm of composition-decomposition-recomposition. He admits previous versions of himself but finds it impossible to escape from this egotism since to do so would be to escape from language itself. So he describes, for instance, Seymour the Oriental expert, and then dismisses his 'somewhat pustulous disquisition' on Seymour's poetry before moving on to a new tack. His monologue (his 'fool's soliloquy' as he calls it at one point) constantly makes gestures towards his subject, but the biographical data about the Glass family are repeatedly superseded by comments which remind the reader of the immediate present, the now of narration; Seymour as subject even becomes assimilated into the narrator's own self-consciousness as a critic of his short stories.

In this rôle he is inseparable from the narrator's critical (and usually hostile) attitude to his own sentences, an attitude that leads him to exclaim 'let me not screen every damned sentence, for once in my life, or I'm through again' (p. 122). Just as the narrator breaks his brother down into different Seymours or into different physical details (hair, nose, etc.), so he divides himself into two rôles—the describer and the critic, constantly claiming a mock-reluctance to divulge information. Consistent with its own self-consciousness the narrative does not conclude but ends with a discussion of the impossibility of endings.

This novella is Salinger's most experimental work and one which skilfully converts his characters' anxieties about their identity into problems of fictional representation. The narrator is alert to a critical charge repeatedly brought against Salinger's Glass fiction—that he is trying to induce a mood of reverence in the reader—and this time attempts portrayals of Seymour from different partial angles. Now Seymour becomes interesting not from any insistent guru-like status, but because he eludes portrayal, because the reader cannot quite locate the referent of his name.

Seymour—An Introduction represents a fictional extreme beyond which Salinger cannot go, but it is not the last novella to deal with the Glass family. In 1965 Salinger published *Hapworth 16, 1924*, essentially an extended footnote to the series.[23] It is a fictive transcript of a letter written by Seymour in 1924 to his family from summer camp, edited and transcribed by Buddy. This novella is somewhat staid coming after *Raise High* which complicates chronology and narration to show how Seymour eludes explanation, and after *Seymour—An Introduction* where a scepticism about the efficacy of narration feeds Salinger's one work of meta-fiction. The latter narrative is worthy of Beckett in its repeated gestures towards representation which are immediately followed by destructive dismissals.

In *Hapworth 16, 1924* Salinger has returned to a more conventional literary form (the epistle) where a single document becomes the whole narrative, suggesting that, as Eberhard Alsen points out, Salinger's audience has contracted down to the Glass family itself.[24] *Seymour—An Introduction* brings into question all texts about the Glass family, so that a return to conventional coherence looks like an act of bad faith. Not only that. The very fiction of publishing a letter suggests a presumption of importance in the subject, but the letter is written in a most turgid style (grotesque for a child aged 7!) which Seymour admits but continues. The attempted evocation of precocious wisdom actually becomes a supercilious self-important account of the other children, the attendants and the camp routines. In all of Salinger's six published novellas length is used for quite different purposes—to allow an ironic narrative sequence to take its course, to develop the implications of a specific situation (*Franny*), to unfold a brief sequence of events relating to Seymour (*Raise High*), to reveal the Glass family (*Zooey*), and to reflect on the actual processes of literary composition (*Seymour—An Introduction*). Here the main point of length seems to be self-display. Seymour disingenuously admits that he is writing a 'very long, boring letter', but presses on regardless, even finishing with a list of books he wants borrowed from the local library. *Hapworth 16, 1924* demonstrates all too clearly Salinger's difficulties with his central character. Seymour simply does not live up to his inflated presentation by the rest of his family. No character could. The use of the Glass family, which goes so far to explain the particular themes and methods of Salinger's novellas, has ended as a pretext for repetition.

159

NOTES

1. Irving Howe 'The Salinger Cult', *Celebration and Attacks* (London: André Deutsch, 1979), p. 95; Leslie Fiedler, 'Up from Adolescence', *Partisan Review*, 29 (Winter 1962), 128; Frank Kermode, 'One Hand Clapping', *Continuities* (London: Routledge Kegan Paul, 1968), p. 195; Alfred Kazin, 'The Along Generation', in Marcus Klein (ed.), *The American Novel Since World War II* (New York: Fawcett, 1969), pp. 120–21.
2. Malcolm Bradbury, *The Modern American Novel* (Oxford: Oxford University Press, 1983), pp. 145–46.
3. There is evidence within *Hapworth 16, 1924* (Salinger's last published novella) that he was planning to pair it with a story about a party. It is rumoured that this story was actually submitted to the *New Yorker* and then withdrawn.
4. *The Inverted Forest, The Complete Uncollected Stories* n.p. [1974], Vol. 2, 19. This work was first published in *Cosmopolitan* (December 1947).
5. *The Inverted Forest*, p. 40.
6. Mary Doyle Springer, *Forms of the Modern Novella* (Chicago: University of Chicago Press, 1975), p. 12. Warren French, one of the few critics to have noticed this novella, sees it as an allegory of the artist's burden (*J. D. Salinger* (Indianapolis: Bobbs-Merrill, 1976), pp. 66–76). One problem with this reading is that it would privilege Ford as protagonist.
7. *Franny and Zooey* (Harmondsworth: Penguin Books, 1964), p. 15.
8. Daniel Seitzman, 'Salinger's "Franny": Homoerotic Imagery', *American Imago*, 22 (1965), p.62.
9. *The Way of a Pilgrim*, trans. R.M. French (New York: Seabury Press, [1974]), p.10
10. John Updike, '*Franny and Zooey*', *Assorted Prose* (New York: Fawcett, 1969), p.182.
11. William Maxwell, ' J. D.Salinger', *Book-of-the-Month Club News*, 7 (1951), 6.
12. Howard Nemerov, 'Composition and Fate in the Short Novel', *Poetry and Fiction: Essays* (New Brunswick, N. J.: Rutgers University Press, 1963), p. 236.
13. Daniel Seitzman, 'Therapy and Antitherapy in Salinger's "Zooey" ', *American Imago*, 25 (1968), 140–62.
14. A useful discussion of Peale's exploitation of mass-marketing techniques in the postwar period can be found in Donald Meyer's *The Positive Thinkers* (New York: Anchor, 1960), Ch. xxi.
15. Seitzman (op. cit., pp. 150–51) discusses the complex symbolism of the Fat Lady.
16. Warren French, op. cit., p. 143. His distinction between telling and showing is taken from Wayne C. Booth's *The Rhetoric of Fiction*, but hardly relevant here. A guiding principle of Salinger's Glass fiction is that particular members of the family should bear witness.
17. Eberhard Alsen, *Salinger's Glass Stories as a Composite Novel* (Troy, N.Y.: Whitstow, 1983), p. 109.

18. *Raise High the Roofbeam, Carpenter* and *Seymour: An Introduction* (Harmondsworth: Penguin Books, 1964), p. 26.
19. Bernice and Sanford Goldstein, ' "Seymour: An Introduction": Writing As Discovery', *Studies in Short Fiction*, 7 (Spring 1970), p. 249.
20. Salinger's conservative and aloof attitude to the Beats is echoed without the saving grace of the former's witty style by Anthony West who reviewed *The Dharma Bums* in the *New Yorker* for 1 November, 1958: 'As a Zen Buddhist who badly wants to be a Buddha, Mr. Kerouac is even more of an aesthete, and even less of an artist, than he was a hipster—a white bourgeois bohemian pretending just as hard as he could to be a Negro rebel' (p. 164).
21. John O. Lyons, 'The Romantic Style of Salinger's "Seymour: An Introduction" ', *Wisconsin Studies in Contemporary Literature*, 4 (Winter 1963), 64.
22. Ihab Hassan, 'Almost the Voice of Silence: The Later Novelettes of J. D. Salinger', *Wisconsin Studies in Contemporary Literature*, 4 (Winter 1963), 6, 14.
23. Published in the *New Yorker* (19 June 1965).
24. Alsen, op.cit., p. 94.

9

Some Versions of Real: The Novellas of Saul Bellow

by MICHAEL K. GLENDAY

1

> One of my themes is the American denial of real reality, our
> devices for evading it, our refusal to face what is all too obvious
> and palpable.[1]

So, in a discussion of his latest novel, *The Dean's December*
(1982), Saul Bellow speaks of an abiding concern in his fiction—the escapism of Americans, their refusal to face squarely
the 'real reality' upon which national and individual life, as he
sees it, must be founded. He has always stressed this escapist
tendency as a worrisome hallmark of the national psyche, a trait
the narrator of *The Dean's December* calls nothing less than 'the
American moral crisis'. Given the crisis, 'the first act of morality
[is] to disinter the reality, retrieve reality, dig it out from the
trash.'[2] And 'retrieving reality' is nowhere more sharply present
as a concern than in his two early novellas *Dangling Man* (1944)
and *Seize the Day* (1957) and in his return to the form with *What
Kind of Day Did You Have?* (1984).

Perhaps the very intensity and concentration of the novella
form accentuates Bellow's concern in this regard, especially
since, as critics have noted, his longer fiction is occasionally
weakened by his 'metaphysical garrulity'.[3] Though his eminence
has tended to rest upon full-length fictions such as *Augie March*
(1954) and *Herzog* (1965), Bellow has always given notice that

he has been an adept in the art of short fiction as his collection *Him with his Foot in his Mouth and Other Stories* (1984) testifies. As Bellow observed in the 1950s, the business of the writer is not only to take the nature of reality as theme and subject, but also to use the art of fiction as a tool to cut through towards ultimate recognition of that subject:

> to find enduring intuitions of what things are real and what things are important. His business is with these enduring recognitions which have the power to recognize occasions of suffering or occasions of happiness, in spite of all distortions and blearing.[4]

The novella, in Bellow's hands, then, serves as a tool with an especially sharp cutting edge, one that enables him to discover those 'enduring recognitions' of reality with fewer impediments, without the 'distortions and blearing' which sometimes encumber the expression of the same theme in parts of his longer fiction. His use of the shorter form allows him to exploit the localizing incident more effectively, and the plenitude of ideas—often predominating the novels to the detriment of plot and story—is subordinate to the dramatic capacity of such incidents. In the account which follows I want to focus essentially on two novellas, *Seize the Day* and *What Kind of Day Did You Have?*—early and late work respectively—to pursue Bellow's preoccupation with 'obvious and palpable' reality and the devices of 'distortion and blearing' which too often come between Americans and this fundamental recognition 'of what things are real'.

To discuss 'reality' in connection with fiction is, to be sure, to enter a loaded literary minefield. For what else has been at the centre of its concerns, form, philosophy or very purpose? But in Bellow's case, so often and explicitly has he made it the actual *theme* of his work, that it assumes an even greater importance than usual. Reality, in one key sense, is not at all problematic for him: it is there, 'obvious and palpable'. Also, there is very little in Bellow's work to show any trace of that philosophical scepticism about the nature of reality which has so characterized the postmodern literary aesthetic over recent years.[5] There have been few modern American writers quite so vigorous, or persistent, in getting it down upon the page—for all his reputation as an 'ideas' writer Bellow is still a sturdy, unremitting and circumstantial 'realist'. I have said that he uses the novella as a form of fiction that cuts through towards such reality. As a realist, a large part of his own self-appointed brief has been to reflect contemporary data in all its barbarism, the urban killing fields of Chicago—'many, many square miles of civil Passchendaele or Somme'[6]—to make 'the real world realer' and to confront its perversities.[7]

But Bellow, in his Nobel Prize address, acknowledges also that the writer must go beyond documentation, must penetrate towards the essentially real: 'Only art penetrates what pride, passion, intelligence, and habit erect on all sides—the seeming realities of this world.'[8] In the embrace of these 'seeming realities', Americans above all have tended to become chronically unmoored, adrift with nothing solid to cling to. Or as Larry Wrangel, in *What Kind of Day Did You Have?* puts it:

> The created souls of people, of the Americans, have been removed. The created soul has been replaced by an artificial one, so there's nothing real that human beings can refer to when they judge any matter for themselves.[9]

2

Wedged between the stylistic extroversions of *The Adventures of Augie March* and *Henderson the Rain King*, *Seize the Day*, as Marvin Mudrick has observed, still tastes like 'the real pastrami between two thick slices of American store bread'.[10] The members of the Royal Swedish Academy evidently shared Mudrick's taste when they singled out the novella for special mention in Bellow's Nobel Prize citation. Even the Bellow-baiting Mailer grudgingly threw a bouquet in the direction of the book as a tribute to its 'surprisingly beautiful ending', the 'first indication for me that Bellow is not altogether hopeless on the highest level'.[11]

A good deal of critical debate has, perhaps understandably, centred upon the final scene of *Seize the Day*, with some critics arguing that the tears shed by Tommy Wilhelm are ones that signify a new enlightenment for him.[12] Others have contended that the rhetorical flourish of the novella's ending cannot disguise Bellow's inability to resolve narrative tensions satisfactorily.[13] My own view is that the ending is perfectly compatible as a response to, and a culmination of, Bellow's searing condemnation of American 'reality'—the subject of *Seize the Day*. It also provides a perfect example of Bellow's skill in the novella form, his use of the dramatic incident as a means of heightening and intensifying thematic concerns. The reader has been led, from the very start, to anticipate a climactic ending, a resolution to suspenseful elements of the narrative:

> he was aware that his routine was about to break up and he sensed that a huge trouble long presaged but till now formless was due. Before evening, he'd know.[14]

Bellow uses the brevity of the novella to embody these tensions, to lead inexorably towards Tommy's convulsive *cri de coeur*. His fiction is full of anguished and heart-torn individuals, but surely none so full of anguish and heartache as Tommy. One of the main reasons for this must be due in large part to the sharp and unremitting awfulness of Tommy's 'day', undiluted in novella medium. The reader is as permanently conscious of Tommy's suffering as Tommy himself; the third-person narrator maintains that intimacy, refusing the reader any remission at all.

This narrator stresses throughout the horrific price Tommy pays for his physical appearance ('fair-haired hippopotamus'), his *gaucherie*, his failure in the business world, and his lack of emotional reserve. Mainstream reality in America is still—as Joseph of *Dangling Man* puts it in the first paragraph of Bellow's first novel—dominated by 'hardboiled-dom'. According to this regimen one has to be a tough guy, possessed of a mind defined by Henry Adams more than a century ago as 'a cutting instrument, practical, economical, sharp and direct'.[15] The narrator mocks Tommy's efforts to keep up appearances of capability, telling us that Tommy

> had once been an actor—no, not quite, an extra—and he knew what acting should be. Also, he was smoking a cigar, and when a man is smoking a cigar, wearing a hat, he has an advantage; it is harder to find out how he feels. (p. 7)

Tommy knows the ground rules, knows how he is expected to behave, having been taught by his father how, despite 'bad luck, weariness, weakness, and failure' he must still affect a low-key tone, must 'sound gentlemanly, low-voiced, tasteful' (p. 15). He knows also the rules that govern American reality, but always loses the game.

> I am an idiot. I have no reserve ... I talk. I must ask for it.
> Everybody wants to have intimate conversations, but the smart
> fellows don't give out, only the fools. (p. 43)

Dr. Adler's repudiation of his son is justified to some extent.
Indeed Bellow has carefully prepared a case for the doctor's
perception of Tommy as a slob, a miscreant, a maladroit
bungler with an unerring talent for taking the wrong road. Dr.
Adler, then, as has been argued, 'is right, when his slovenly,
failure-ridden son comes on his knees, begging, to both feel and
articulate his disgust. He is right but not human.'[16]

And this is Bellow's subject in *Seize the Day*: not Tommy's
pathos but all those, such as his father and Tamkin—the
primary 'reality-instructor'[17] of the novel—by whose example
he seems such a misfit. Such a reality, as Martin Amis has
recently pointed out in connection with Bellow's fiction, 'is not
a given but a gift, a talent, an accomplishment, an objective'.[18]
Whereas Joseph of *Dangling Man* sets out in knowledgeable
defiance of a prime commandment of American reality—'if
you have difficulties grapple with them silently'[19]—Tommy's
pathos derives from his unexamined acceptance of this axiom.
His tears at the end are an expression of his inability to live
within a reality that is contemptuous of their shedding.

In one of his acute culture-readings in *In the American Grain*,
William Carlos Williams denunciates the 'coldness and skill'
which serve as an accepted part of American manners:

> Who is open to injuries? Not Americans. Get hurt; you're a fool.
> The only hero is he who is not hurt. We have no feeling for the
> tragic. Let the sucker who fails get his. What's tragic in that?
> That's funny! To hell with him. He didn't make good, that's all.[20]

Years after the publication of *Seize the Day*, Bellow spoke in an
interview of his belief in the necessity of emotional display, and
of the hardboiled American ethos that condemns such emotional
release:

> Is feeling nothing but self-indulgence? ... When people release
> emotion, they so often feel like imposters. By restraining them-
> selves, they claim credit for a barren kind of honesty ... Nothing
> is gained by letting yourself go among people who hate such
> letting go.[21]

Tommy Wilhelm is by far the most vulnerable of Bellow's major characters. Whereas other Bellow heroes like Albert Corde, Moses Herzog, and Charlie Citrine[22] realize the prudence of closing the valves of feeling in public, Tommy has neither the intelligence nor the guile to develop any strategies of concealment. He is 'the sucker who fails', and *Seize the Day* is the story of how America sends him to hell, how he 'gets his' from America's hardboiled and heartless.

In the novella's final scene, Bellow's stress falls upon Tommy 'hidden' in the centre of a crowd of mourners. Though it is true that Tommy cries openly, he is in the most crucial sense as concealed as ever, 'protected by the occasion'[23] of the funeral rite so that the onlookers are never truly aware of the nature of his grief. Instead of being outraged, embarrassed, or moved by that grief, these onlookers are merely curious, or, more significantly, envious—' "It must be somebody real close to carry on so". "Oh my, oh my! To be mourned like that", said one man . . . with wide, glinting, jealous eyes' (p. 125). In a culture in which real feeling has apparently atrophied, the generous tears of Tommy Wilhelm turn him into a bizarre celebrity.

Ironically, too, Tommy is made to seem a dramatic embodiment of Bellow's idea that 'when people release emotion, they so often feel like imposters', as one mourner wonders whether Tommy was 'perhaps the cousin from New Orleans they were expecting' (p. 125). So this final scene demonstrates not 'the possibility of communion', not Tommy's newly-found connections with the city's crowd, but rather his awful isolation, his emotional release figured as a sinking downwards 'deeper than sorrow' towards extravagant oblivion. The oblivion is 'great and happy' because it serves simultaneously as both an expression and extinction of self. American reality has broken him, denied him, hounded him and fleeced him. Finally ('Wilhelm was moved forward by the pressure of the crowd . . . carried from the street into the chapel') it brings him face to face with the look of death. But Tommy sees beyond the reality of appearances:

> Now at last he was with it, after the end of all distractions, and when his flesh was no longer flesh. And by this meditative look Tommy was so struck that he could not go away . . . On the surface, the dead man with his formal shirt and his tie and silk lapels and his powdered skin looked so proper; only a little

beneath so—black, Wilhelm thought, so fallen in the eyes. Standing a little apart, Wilhelm began to cry. (pp. 124-25)

Tamkin is in some ways the major character of the novella,[24] no less than a prototype in Bellow's fiction. He also bears a striking resemblance to the protean Rinehart of Ellison's *Invisible Man* or the adaptive Milo Minderbinder of *Catch-22*, not to mention numerous similar figures in Thomas Pynchon's fiction. He is also the forerunner of Valentine Gersbach in *Herzog* and Dewey Spangler in *The Dean's December*, as well as of Victor Wulpy in *What Kind of Day?* Like Gersbach, Tamkin comes over as the self-proclaimed poet who also 'put himself forward as the keen mental scientist' (p.67). Both Dr. Adler (described as 'a fine old scientist') and Tamkin, who gambled 'scientifically', are associated with an anti-humanistic rationalism which will reappear in Bellow's fiction in increasingly nasty forms until given its baleful apotheosis in *The Dean's December*. There, we are told by Bellow's narrator, that we may indeed have reached a stage wherein 'science had drawn all the capacity for deeper realizations out of the rest of mankind and monopolized it. This left everyone else in a condition of great weakness.'[25] Like Spangler and Wulpy, Tamkin is a rhetorician who has no purpose 'except to talk' (p. 99). And just as Albert Corde makes the mistake of unburdening himself to Spangler in Budapest, Tamkin finds Tommy willing prey. Following his rejection by his father Tommy stumbles into Tamkin's orbit, feeling that there at least he would find one who could 'sympathise with me' and try 'to give me a hand' (p. 14).

It is of course Tamkin who voices the novella's *carpe diem* ethos; he is the successful predator, perfectly adapted to the jungle of the American metropolis, 'the end of the world, with its complexity and machinery, bricks and tubes, wires and stones, holes and heights' (p. 89). Amidst this frightening perplexity, Tommy prays that Tamkin will show him the way, 'give him some useful advice and transform his life' (p. 78). But like Wulpy's mistress Katrina ('an average Dumb Dora'), so Tommy knows he is 'a sucker for people who talk about the deeper things of life' (p. 74). Tamkin, however, for all his rhetorical composure, is not in truth that complex a being. Bellow's narrator allows us to see Tamkin in much the same way as we eventually see Gersbach of *Herzog*—'not an individual, but a fragment, a piece broken off from the mob'.[26] We feel, too, the underlying terror that buoys up Tamkin's masquerade as well as feeling the slightest bit of sympathy for the very real sense in which Tamkin is as much the prey of 'the world's business' (p. 41) as Tommy:

> his face did not have much variety. Talking always about spontaneous emotion and open receptors and free impulses he was about as expressive as a pincushion. When his hypnotic spell failed, his big underlip made him look weakminded. Fear stared from his eyes, sometimes, so humble as to make you sorry for him. Once or twice Wilhelm had seen that look. Like a dog, he thought. (pp. 104-5)

The remote but detectable resemblance to the eyes of the dead man in the final scene ('on the surface . . . so proper; only a little beneath so—black, Wilhelm thought, so fallen in the eyes') is a chilling touch, for Tamkin of course has no being, no personality, no soul. He succeeds because of his protean capacities ('Funny but unfunny. True but false. Casual but laborious, Tamkin was' (p. 71)) and because of his fake profundity which creates a reality beyond comprehension, so that

> listening to the doctor when he was so strangely factual, Wilhelm had to translate his words into his own language, and he could not translate fast enough or find terms to fit what he had heard. (p. 73)

But in Bellow's trenchant vision of American reality as nightmare, this confusion of language and meaning is one that extends to embrace the entire gamut of knowledge, and knowledgeability, to lead modern America towards the vortex reality of absolute unintelligibility where solipsism alone reigns:

> You had to translate and translate, explain and explain, back and forth, and it was the punishment of hell itself not to understand or be understood, not to know the crazy from the sane, the wise from the fools, the young from the old or the sick from the well. The fathers were no fathers and the sons no sons. You had to talk with yourself in the daytime and reason with yourself at night. Who else was there to talk to in a city like New York? (pp. 89-90)

Tamkin is at once creator, beneficiary and victim of this state of affairs. He feeds on the likes of Tommy without scruple.

169

Bellow's physical description of Tamkin emphasizes the animal in him as well as the deceiver, and there are insinuations too of Mephistophelian grossness and carnality.[27] The image of Tamkin's twisted anatomy may be the analogue of his perversion of the natural which is his stock-in-trade. 'If you were to believe Tamkin ... everybody in the hotel had a mental disorder, a secret history, a concealed disease ... every public figure had a character-neurosis' (p. 69). And commensurate with the suggestion that Tamkin embodies a kind of barely concealed, devilish bestiality, is his view of reality as hell, an infernal pit of pain and suffering:

> Wilhelm said, 'But this means that the world is full of murderers. So it's not the world. It's a kind of hell.'
> 'Sure,' the doctor said. 'At least a kind of purgatory. You walk on the bodies. They are all around. I can hear them cry *de profundis* and wring their hands. I hear them, poor human beasts. I can't help hearing.' (p. 77)

In its depiction of dissociation and dissolution, of Dr. Adler's well-dressed affability and heartlessness triumphing over his son's despair, of Tamkin's high-powered mountebankery exploiting that despair, *Seize the Day* warns of the crisis afflicting American reality. Wilhelm's 'reality' is made up of despair, confusion, loneliness and failure; this is his 'real reality', the bottom line, 'obvious and palpable' in the suffering it inflicts upon him. Because they cannot, or will not, take account of this reality, having built up defences of 'seeming realities', those who could have taken the elementary moral, human step—his father, his sister, family and friends—hasten Tommy's demise. As Larry Wrangel remarks in *What Kind of Day Did You Have?*, 'what's really real is the unseen convulsion under the apparitions' (p.113). Perhaps this is the kindest view to take of all those who deny Tommy's 'real reality', to say that they simply do not see it. But the price for such blindness is the highest man can pay, a Faustian price—their souls removed, to be 'replaced by an artificial one, so there's nothing real that human beings can refer to when they try to judge any matter for themselves'.

That all of these thematic concerns are carried within the novella format is a tribute to Bellow's ability to make that format more capacious than its slender frame would seem to imply. The tribute is the greater when we consider that unlike Hemingway in *The Old Man and the Sea*, or James's *The Beast in the Jungle*, Bellow does not rely upon symbolical properties to give narrative depth. Instead the profundity and intensity of his themes are carried in and through such things as the immaculately rendered linear plot—enhanced in terms of suspense and drama by its diurnal span—and here the novella's brevity makes it a propitious vessel; and there is also the presence in this novella of some of Bellow's best writing: succinct, lyrical, evocative, and in these ways a revelation to all those readers put off by the prosiness of the longer fiction.

3

What Kind of Day Did You Have?, Bellow's latest novella, consolidates his vision of American reality as I have been seeking to describe it. Again, Bellow chooses to give this novella the time-scale frame of a single day, an apparently climactic day in the lives of the two central characters. Yet the tale is clearly late-Bellow in many ways. Structurally, and even within the constraints imposed by the form, it is more diffuse, even ending in deliberate anti-climax. One feels the ending might have been more pointedly accomplished, especially after a consideration of the virtues of *Seize the Day*, yet the conclusion of the later novella contains muted epiphanies which perhaps required the understated ending. Victor Wulpy, the character who towers over the story, amounts to one of Bellow's most biting satirical portraits of the American intellectual. Though Tamkin is his antecedent, Wulpy is physically and mentally more formidable, 'a kind of tyrant in thought' (p. 96). Fortunately, the novella's concision imposes its own discipline upon that tyrannical display, though Wulpy is, in the course of the story itself, forced to consider the nature of his tyrannical thoughts.

Wulpy's character had been predicted in Bellow's novels of the '60s; Herzog, for instance, has been a witness to man's preparing to assume the mantle of his 'future condition', a condition of amoral automatism 'free from human dependency'.[28] Artur Sammler, too, faces up to the same dehumanized projection of the race, knowing that the day of the 'old-fashioned sitting sage'[29] is over. The day of Wulpy, the shuttle-intellectual, has arrived.

His very name, Victor, confirms his peerless command—'such a face, such stature; without putting it on, he was so commanding that he often struck people as being a king' (p. 65).

Into his kingdom comes Katrina, who 'had been raised to consider herself a nitwit' (p. 66). Her home-life is in a mess; she is in the middle of an 'ugly' divorce, and her two young daughters are the subject of a custody wrangle. This broken family and its *anomie* give us the damning backdrop against which the events and relationships of the novella are played out. As with *Seize the Day*, Bellow exploits the time-span to good effect. The narrative opens with Katrina about to leave her Chicago home and its two daughters, and closes with her return to it after travelling back from Boston with Wulpy. Again the brevity of the novella enhances this pattern; we are, for instance, always aware of the maternal responsibilities Katrina has left behind her in Chicago, indeed this particular abdication of duty becomes a central aspect of the novella's moral design.

What Katrina desires, is what middle-America desires: significance, *gravitas*, a piece of the action, however vicarious or compromising. In a 1975 interview Bellow spoke of this rage for significance in American life:

> Life . . . has become very current-eventish. People think they
> are political when they are immersed in these events—vicari-
> ously. . . . Society is monopolising their brains, and taking their
> souls away from them by this interest, by the news, by spurious
> politics.[30]

Wulpy is Katrina's way-in to this reality. She signs up with him, a babble-king who can connect her to the current of current-events. She needs this like a drug to relieve herself of the boredom of all that her home life entails, since 'when the current stopped, the dullness and depression were worse than ever' (p. 116). By trading in her family for Wulpy she can now share a room with 'the Motherwells and Rauschenbergs and Ashberys and Frankenthalers and . . . leave the local culture creeps grovelling in the dust' (p. 66). The frame of departure and return allows Bellow to use this novella so as to meaningfully enmesh form and subject. We are able to view the object of Katrina's Bostonian flight, to see Wulpy perform his tyrannies (and here it is interesting to note that Bellow needed the extra

172

wordage to do justice to Wulpy's Olympian bearing—the effect could not have been achieved within the smaller compass of a short story), and to receive the challenge posed by the Larry Wrangel character. So we are able to see what she has sacrificed, and what she has sacrificed it for.

The moral design of *What Kind of Day Did You Have?* is similar to that of *Seize the Day*. It is one in which the realities of public life—represented and interpreted by Wulpy, here a kind of Tamkin empowered—are seen to bear down upon, and to be inimical to, the imperatives of personal ethics. In this context, Katrina's children are wordless witnesses of their neglect, hovering in the far background of the story (in the domestic overviews comprising the 'frame' of the story's beginning and end; so in the far background in terms of their mother's 'day' but not at all minimalized by Bellow's narrator, who makes their silent presence so eerily indicting in the important frame areas), 'silent Pearl, wordless Soolie' are forced to ponder their mother's unseemly departure from their wintry Chicago home to Boston and Wulpy's bed.

As so often in Bellow's fiction[31] family ties are an index to the probity of his characters. Because Wulpy is wholly devoid of a moral nature, 'categories like wife, parent, child never could affect his judgement. He could discuss a daughter like any other subject submitted to his concentrated, radiant consideration' (p. 107). However, Victor 'didn't like to speak of kids. He especially avoided discussing her children' (p. 89). He has a daughter whom he calls 'a little bitch'. Her more recent claims to that title have included 'giving her mother sex advice' together with 'the address of a shop where she could read some passages on foreplay' (p. 106). Of course Wulpy never considers the extent to which his own neglect of parental responsibilities have contributed to these violations of the natural, only that such 'facts' seem to him to 'add up to an argument for abortion' (pp. 106-7). For Wulpy, 'insofar as they were nothing but personal, he cared for nobody's troubles' (p. 95). His grotesque blindness to the elemental duties of fatherhood is compounded by Katrina's willingness to accept Wulpy as 'the child . . . which not even my own kids will be with me' and by her acknowledgement that 'as a mother I seem to be an artificial product' (p. 104).

The latter remark as noted earlier anticipates that of the novella's co-star, Larry Wrangel. He correctly exposes the inhumanity of Wulpy's idea-mongering mentality:

> You always set a high value on ideas, Victor. I remember that. Well, I've considered this from many sides, and I am convinced that most ideas are trivial. A thought of the real is also an image of the real; if it's a true thought, it's a true picture and is accompanied by a true feeling. Without this our ideas are corpses. (p. 114)

This confrontation between Wrangel and Wulpy marks the centre point of the tale. He is the only character able to challenge Wulpy, and he does so successfully as Wulpy himself later seems to concede ('there may have been something in what Wrangel said' (p. 147). His attack is aimed at the inhuman abstraction of Wulpy's thinking; in peddling abstractions Wulpy is a 'caricaturist', his shorthand representations causing human beings, in reduction, to be 'represented as *things*' (p. 137). Like Albert Corde, Wrangel argues that this tendency towards abstraction both contributes to, and results from the flight from 'real reality':

> We prefer to have such things served up to us as concepts. We'd rather have them abstract, stillborn, dead. But as long as they don't come to us with some kind of reality, as facts of experience, then all we can have instead of good and evil is . . . concepts. Then we'll never know how the soul is worked on. Then for intellectuals there will be discourse or jargon, while for the public there will be ever more jazzed-up fantasy.[32]

For Bellow, a writer renowned for the intellectual appetite of his work, the above seems an extraordinary indictment of intellectual process. The attack, however is more properly seen as one levelled at what passes for a moral use of such process. Instead of an intellectual response based upon 'facts of experience', minds such as Wulpy's, trained to entertain rather than edify, can only add to the rift between an authentic reality and its public travesty. Bellow's point is that the development of a moral sense depends upon this correspondence between intellect and experience, and that without it there can only be a degeneration of the moral life.

As I noted earlier, there is a subdued epiphany for Katrina at the close of the narrative. But unlike *Seize the Day*, this novella aims more at representing the unleavened slice of life, a life that will continue to be lived—certainly by Wulpy, probably by Katrina—in the way of the narrative's day. Still, even Victor fleetingly realizes—as the small plane carrying them back to Chicago seems about to plummet into Lake Michigan—the force of Wrangel's criticisms and the truth that 'of all that might be omitted in thinking, the worst was to omit your own being' (p. 156). But Bellow is quick to stress the momentary nature of this insight, and the last we see of Wulpy is the picture Katrina has of him 'in the swift, rich men's gilded elevator rushing upward, upward' towards his next public address—'pressed for time . . . all that unfinished mental business to keep him busy forever and forever' (p. 159).

But it is in Katrina's return home that Bellow proves his mastery of the novella form. For it is only at that point that the reader realizes the importance of this territory, and realizes, too, that the narrative had been bound to return there, with its neglected children waiting—and certainly not for the first time—for Katrina's brief interludes of motherhood. The relative brevity of the novella means we have not forgotten their environment, though since leaving it at the beginning of the narrative we have seen how odious is the personality and the life-style for which they have been sacrificed. Katrina finds her house empty and though her initial fear that her children have been taken away by their father proves to be unfounded, there is a terrible irreducible reality—unsullied by any abstraction—in their renunciation of the maternal tie, in their alien self-sufficiency:

> They didn't say, 'Where have you been, Mother?' She was not called upon for any alibis. Their small faces communicated nothing. They did have curious eyes, science-fiction eyes, that dazzled and also threatened from afar . . . Emissaries from another planet, grown from seeds that dropped from outer space, little invaders with iridium in their skulls. (pp. 162–3)

Like Tommy Wilhelm, these innocents are the misfits, without reality in a world of distorted forms—'the fathers no fathers and the sons no sons'. Katrina, self-confessedly an 'artificial' mother, has perpetuated the breed, the nothingness of response and the remoteness in her daughters' eyes being a chilling cause to reflect again upon Wrangel's theory that 'the created souls ... of the Americans have been removed'.

Both novellas are powerful examinations of the extent to which Americans collaborate in this process. And the fact that they are novellas shows how well Bellow is able to explore the potentialities of this bantam form, using its brevity to create effects—of suspense, and of subtle thematic control—not possible in novel or short story. 'To have a soul, to *be* one—that today is a revolutionary defiance of received opinion'[33], Bellow remarked in a recent interview. In such a climate these novellas suggest that the reality of American lives will be one of increasing artificiality, increasing inhumanity.

NOTES

1. Matthew C. Roudané, 'An Interview with Saul Bellow', *Contemporary Literature*, 25 (1974), 270.
2. *The Dean's December* (New York, 1982), p. 123.
3. Tony Tanner, *Saul Bellow* (Edinburgh, 1965), p. 111.
4. 'The Writer and the Audience', *Perspectives*, 9 (Autumn 1954), 12.
5. For a concise and lucid exposition of the postmodern aesthetic and its distinctive literary expression, see David Lodge, *The Modes of Modern Writing: Metaphor, Metonymy, and the Typology of Modern Literature* (London, 1977), pp. 220–45.
6. *The Dean's December*, p. 205.
7. Martin Amis, 'The Moronic Inferno', in his *The Moronic Inferno and Other Visits to America* (London, 1986), p. 10.
8. 'The Nobel Lecture', *American Scholar*, 46 (1977), 321.
9. In *Him with his Foot in his Mouth and Other Stories* (London, 1984), p. 114. All further references are to this edition and will be given after quotations in the text of the essay.
10. 'Who Killed Herzog? Or, Three American Novelists', *University of Denver Quarterly*, 1 (1966), 78.
11. *Advertisements for Myself* (London, 1965), p.402.
12. See, for instance, M. Gilbert Porter, 'The Scene as Image: A Reading of *Seize the Day*', in *Saul Bellow: A Collection of Critical Essays*, edited by Earl Rovit (Englewood Cliffs, New Jersey, 1975), p. 70; Clinton W. Trowbridge, 'Water Imagery in *Seize the Day*', *Critique*, 9, No. 3 (1967), 62–73; and Malcolm Bradbury, *Saul Bellow* (London, 1982), pp. 55–6.
13. See Andrew Waterman, 'Saul Bellow's Ineffectual Angels', in *On the Novel*, edited by B. S. Benedikz (London, 1971), p. 228.
14. *Seize the Day* (Harmondsworth, 1966), p. 7. All further references are to this edition and will be given after quotations in the text of the essay.

15. *The Education of Henry Adams: An Autobiography* (London, 1919), p. 181.
16. Gerald Nelson, 'Tommy Wilhelm', in his *Ten Versions of America* (New York, 1972), p. 135.
17. Saul Bellow, *Herzog* (London, 1965), p. 125.
18. 'Saul Bellow in Chicago', in *The Moronic Inferno*, p. 208.
19. *Dangling Man* (London, 1946), p. 9.
20. *In the American Grain* (London, 1966), p. 180.
21. Maggie Simmons, 'Free to Feel: A Conversation With Saul Bellow', *Quest* (February/March 1979), 32.
22. Of *The Dean's December* (1982), *Herzog* (1965), and *Humboldt's Gift* (1975) respectively.
23. Ray B. West, 'Six Authors in Search of a Hero', *Sewanee Review*, 65 (1957), 505.
24. Bellow has said (Simmons, p. 31) that 'it isn't Tommy Wilhelm . . . that interests me but that crook and phony, Dr. Tamkin.'
25. *The Dean's December*, p.141.
26. *Herzog*, p. 258.
27. See the description of Tamkin on pp. 67-8.
28. *Herzog*, p. 265.
29. *Mr. Sammler's Planet* (London, 1970), p.74.
30. Robert Boyars and others, 'Literature and Culture: An Interview with Saul Bellow', *Salmagundi*, 30 (Summer 1975), 11. And as early as 1963 Bellow was casting doubt even upon the resistance of the stoutest minds when confronted by such omnipresent foes; he wrote then that 'public life, vivid and formless turbulence, news, slogans, mysterious crises, and unreal configurations dissolve coherence in all but the most resistant minds, and even to such minds it is not always a confident certainty that resistance can ever have a positive outcome'. 'Recent American Fiction', *Encounter* 21 (November 1963), 23.
31. Apart from Tommy's neglect by his father, one remembers Herzog's desertion by his wife, Madeleine, and the breakdown of family ties in the relationship between Asa Leventhal and his in-laws in *The Victim* (1947), Henderson and his family in *Henderson the Rain King* (1959), and Joseph and his wife and family in *Dangling Man* (1944).
32. *The Dean's December*, p. 243.
33. Rockwell Gray, Harry White, and Gerald Nemanic, 'Interview with Saul Bellow', *TriQuarterly*, 60 (Spring/Summer 1984), 14.

Notes on Contributors

HAROLD BEAVER has just retired as Professor of American Literature at the University of Amsterdam. He has contributed five editions of Melville and Poe to the Penguin English Library. He has recently collected his essays on American literature in *The Great American Masquerade* (1985) for the Critical Studies Series, and published a study of *Huckleberry Finn* (1987) for the Unwin Critical Library.

MICHAEL GLENDAY taught American literature at the University of Manchester from 1979-83 and is now Senior Lecturer in American Studies at the Liverpool Institute of Higher Education. His previous publications have included essays on Saul Bellow and James Dickey, and his *Saul Bellow and the Decline of Humanism* is scheduled for publication in 1989.

DOROTHY GOLDMAN is Lecturer in Literature at the University of Kent at Canterbury's School of Continuing Education. She has published introductions to Dorothy Canfield's *Her Son's Wife* and *The Brimming Cup* and is presently preparing an edition of Wilkie Collins's *Basil* for World's Classics which, with her essays on Michael Arlen, Fergus Hume and Christianna Brand, reflects her interest in detective fiction.

MICHAEL IRWIN has held lectureships at universities in Poland and Japan and at Smith College in the United States. His published works include *Henry Fielding: The Tentative Realist*, *Picturing: Description and Illusion in the Nineteenth-century Novel*, and two works of fiction *Working Orders* and *Striker*. He is currently Professor of English Literature at the University of Kent.

A. ROBERT LEE is Senior Lecturer in English and American Literature at the University of Kent at Canterbury. He is editor of the Everyman *Moby-Dick* (1975) and of nine previous collections in the Critical Studies Series, among the most recent *Herman Melville: Reassessments* (1984), *Edgar Allan Poe: The Design of Order* (1986),

First-Person Singular: Studies in American Autobiography (1988) and *Scott Fitzgerald: The Promises of Life* (1989). He is the author of a monograph *Black American Fiction Since Richard Wright* (1983) and a wide range of essays on American culture. He broadcasts for B.B.C. radio and is a book-reviewer for the *Listener*.

PETER MESSENT lectures in American Studies at the University of Nottingham, having taught previously at the University of Manchester and at California State University, Sacramento. He has published essays on Kurt Vonnegut and Mark Twain, and edited *Literature of the Occult: A Collection of Critical Essays* and (with Tom Paulin) *Henry James: Selected Tales*.

DAVID SEED teaches American literature at the University of Liverpool. Among his recent publications are articles on Henry James, Thomas Pynchon, I. B. Singer, James Fenimore Cooper, Henry Roth, Ernest Hemingway and William Faulkner. His book-length study of Thomas Pynchon appeared in 1987 and he is currently at work on a study of Joseph Heller.

SHARON SHALOO, a lecturer in English at the University of Lowell, Massachusetts, is completing a study of the interplay of autobiography and fiction in the works of Edith Wharton.

DAVID TIMMS is Lecturer in American Literature at the University of Manchester. He is author of *Philip Larkin* (1973) and has written articles on contemporary British poetry, Conrad, Hawthorne and Henry James.

Index

Index

Irving, Washington, 8

James, Henry, 8, 13–29; *An International Episode*, 20; *Daisy Miller*, 9, 15–17; *In the Cage*, 9, 13, 23–8; *Pandora*, 18–19; *Roderick Hudson*, 110; *The Aspen Papers*, 98; *The Beast in the Jungle*, 9, 22–3, 105; *The Birthplace*, 13, 20; *The Death of the Lion*, 98, 104; *The Figure in the Carpet*, 14, 20, 21, 23; *The Pension Beaurepas*, 13; *The Turn of the Screw*, 9, 14, 21, 98
Jameson, Frederic, 113, 123
Jarrell, Randall, 103
Jones, Anne Goodwyn: *Tomorrow is Another Day: The Woman Writer in the South, 1859–1936*, 124, 125, 128
Jones, James: *From Here to Eternity*, 33

Kafka, Franz, 87, 91
Kantor, MacKinlay: *Andersonville*, 32
Keats, John, 109
Kierkegaard, Søren, 92
Kleist, Heinrich, 8

Lawrence, D. H.: *St. Mawr*, 98
Leavis, F. R., 98
Lukacs, Georg, 104
Lytle, Andrew, 11; *Alchemy*, 117

Mailer, Norman, 33, 119; *The Naked and the Dead*, 33, 119
Marx Brothers, 89
McCullers, Carson, 11, 124; *Reflections in a Golden Eye*, 132, 134; *The Ballad of the Sad Café*, 132–34
Melville, Herman, 8, 32; *Battle Pieces*, 32; *Billy Budd, Sailor*, 9, 40; *Israel Potter: or, Fifty Years of Exile*, 9; *Moby-Dick*, 8
Mitchell, Margaret: *Gone with the Wind*, 32
Monet, Claude, 34
Moore, George, 87, 89
Morris, William, 71

Nabokov, Vladimir: *Lolita*, 157; *Pale Fire*, 97
Norris, Frank, 33

Odyssey, The, 32
Owen, Wilfred, 33
Ozick, Cynthia, 83

Parker, Hershel, 34
Perelman, S. J., 89
Pisarro, Camille, 34
Poe, Edgar Allan, 8, 68, 71, 72, 73, 77; 'The

Philosophy of Furniture', 73, 82
Poirier, Richard, 100
Porter, Katherine Anne, 11, 124, 125; *Noon Wine*, 128; *Old Mortality*, 126–31, 135; *Pale Horse, Pale Rider*, 128; *The Cracked Looking Glass*, 128; *The Leaning Tower*, 128
Proust, Marcel, 70

Renoir, Pierre-Auguste, 34
Rosenberg, Isaac, 33
Rossetti, Dante Gabriel, 71
Ruskin, John, 71

Salinger, J. D., 11, 139–61; 'A Perfect Day for Bananafish', 148; *Franny and Zooey*, 11, 142–54, 156, 159; *Hapworth 16, 1924*, 158–59; 'Last Day of the Last Furlough', 148; 'Pretty Mouth and Green my Eyes', 143; *Raise High the Roof Beam, Carpenters*, 140, 154–56; *Seymour— An Introduction*, 140, 157–58, 159; 'This Sandwich has no Mayonnaise', 148
Scholes, Robert: *Towards a Poetics of Fiction*, 109
Schwitters, Kurt, 89, 91
Shakespeare, William, 7; *Hamlet*, 91
Sherman, William T., 32
Sidney, Sir Philip: *Apologie for Poetrie*, 7
Springer, Mary Doyle: *Forms of the Modern Novella*, 98
Staël, Madame de: *Corinne*, 141
Stephens, Alexander H., 32
Sterne, Laurence: *Tristram Shandy*, 97
Styron, William, 11; *The Long March*, 119–20
Swift, Jonathan, 87

Taylor, Cora, 31
Thoreau, Henry David, 8; *Walden*, 8
Tolstoy, Leo, 33
Treichler, Paula A., 48, 57
Twain, Mark, 32; *Huckleberry Finn*, 87; 'The Private History of a Campaign that Failed', 32

Updike, John, 119, 147

Virgil, 32
Voltaire, 87
Vonnegut, Kurt, 33

Warren, Robert Penn, 11; *The Circus in the Attic*, 118, 135
Wells, H. G., 106
Welty, Eudora, 11, 124; *The Ponder Heart*, 125, 131–32

182

Index